# Carl-Auer-Systeme

# Farewell

**Bert Hellinger**

Family Constellations with Descendants
of Victims and Perpetrators

Translated by Coleen Beaumont

**2003**

Published by Carl-Auer-Systeme Verlag: **www.carl-auer.de**
Please order our catalogue:
**Carl-Auer-Systeme Verlag**
**Weberstrasse 2**
**69120 Heidelberg**
**Germany**

Cover: WSP Design, Heidelberg
Coverpainting: "Peace – Burial at Sea" by William Turner, 1842
Printed by Koninklijke Wöhrmann B. V., Zutphen
Printed in The Netherlands

ISBN 3-89670-395-1

Title of the original edition:
„Der Abschied. Nachkommen von Tätern und Opfern stellen ihre Familien"
© 1998 by Carl-Auer-Systeme Verlag

Bibliographic information published by Die Deutsche Bibliothek
Die Deutsche Bibliothek lists this publication in the Deutsche Nationalbibliografie;
detailed bibliographic data is available in the Internet at http://dnb.ddb.de.

# Contents

# Prologue

Over the years, I have repeatedly encountered the legacy of the Nazi era in the effects on participants in courses. The descendants' entanglements in the fate of the victims and the guilt of the perpetrators have consequences for their present families and have caused suffering in these later generations. In the constellations set up in these courses, the victims and the perpetrators are brought back into the family where they provide support for relieving the suffering of the current family. This book is a documentation of such encounters, relating the authentic stories that have been not so much told as dramatically portrayed by those who have been directly affected. Through the family constellations, we pick up the threads of the story at the point where they were so brutally broken off, and we hear from the survivors as well as the dead, the guilty as well as the victims, and from the descendants of them all.

The family constellation is a therapeutic method in which the client selects people from those present to represent the members of his or her family. The representatives are positioned in relationship to one another according to the client's inner feelings. When the representatives are placed in position, they inexplicably begin to have unfamiliar feelings and reactions, as if they were the persons they represent. The accuracy of this as a reflection of the actual person can only be verified for those who are still living, of course, and not for those who have already died. In any case, the observable effects suggest that the dead are in some way represented, heard, and experienced through their representatives. It is as if an inter-dependence exists between the living and the dead which crosses the boundary of death.

When the dead are allowed to participate in this way, it becomes clear to the current family members that their own feelings cannot be projected onto the dead. The dead participate in guilt and fate on a different level, which overrides our mortal feelings of grief or need for atonement. Life and death, as well as guilt and innocence, are determined by powers that do not function according to our desires or specifications; instead, they respond to an order that reaches far beyond the fate of any single individual.

The dead are in harmony with this larger order of things, at least as far as we can see in the constellations; and the descendants of victims and perpetrators alike find support and comfort when the dead are allowed to speak. People grieving secretly hope to undo what cannot be undone, a process which permits no end to that which has happened and continues to work through generation after generation. There is no healing brought about by descendants sharing the same fate as the dead, and the dead do not ask for such atonement and suffering. The dead seem to be benign towards the descendants, even the children and grandchildren of perpetrators, and do not demand that innocent children take on the guilt of their ancestors.

This book is offered as a contribution towards the process of reconciliation between victims and their murderers, and as such, is also part of the process of reconciliation between Germans and Jews, and between Christians and Jews. In view of this focus, I have included the text of a lecture entitled *Christians and Jews, Germans and Jews– Healing in the Soul*.

The individual encounters are presented here in chronological order; this also reflects a development in my own experience and actions over time. Each instance, however, is complete in itself and can be read separately. Names have been changed to protect the privacy of course participants. Diagrams of the constellations are provided so the reader can visually follow the step-by-step developments in the constellation as well as the dialogue. Readers who are not familiar with family constellations will need to spend some time getting used to decoding the diagrams and visualizing the look of a constellation. Anyone who has difficulty following the constellations can begin with the summaries provided at the beginning of each chapter. These describe the background and the steps taken towards resolution. General comments made during and at the end of constellations will also help with orientation and illuminate the actual proceedings.

I offer this book to all those who have been directly or indirectly affected. Together with them, I bow down before the dead victims and remain silent as they speak. The perpetrators also belong to the world of the dead, and I look at them together with their victims, and make no attempt to step between them. When I die, I shall join them all.

*Bert Hellinger*

## Acknowledgements

My respect and acknowledgement go first and foremost to the descendants of the victims and the perpetrators who have participated in the constellations. Their courage has given me the courage to confront guilt and fate, and to seek resolutions. In the presence of the dead, and with their blessings, resolutions can be found that allow the children and grandchildren to say farewell and to turn with openness to the lives they have been given.

Many people have made valuable suggestions and corrections in the preparation of this documentation, and I give my thanks to them all.

A special thanks to Colleen Beaumont for providing the English translation as well as helpful suggestions for the development of the English edition.

*Bert Hellinger*

# Christian/Jewish German/Jewish Healing in the Soul

*Presented by Bert Hellinger at the Third International Congress for Family and Human Systems Constellations, Würzburg, Germany May 1–4, 2001*

The title of my talk is *Christian/Jewish German/Jewish Healing in the Soul*. What I mean by soul in this context is the soul of Christians and the soul of the Germans. In view of the suffering of the Jewish people during the Nazi era, I am addressing this issue specifically in terms of its impact on the souls of Germans, as distinguished from Christians in general.

## THE CHOSEN AND THE REJECTED

The concept of God's chosen people plays a central role in the souls of both Christians and Jews. The Christians took over this image from the Jews, and subsequently identified themselves as the new chosen people. As a result, they viewed the Jewish people as a rejected people, abandoned by God. The image of a chosen people implies that God prefers one group of people above others, and elevates this group over all other peoples and empowers them to rule in his name.

How could such an image of God find a place in our souls? Can we even talk about God here? Such a God, who chooses and abandons, is frightening, because even those chosen live in fear of being cast out at any time. These are images that come from the depths of the soul – first from the soul of each individual, and then from the great depths of that soul shared by the larger group. The images of being chosen and abandoned arise from this common soul, and are elevated to a heavenly status where they appear to lie above us as something godly, something to be feared. Those who consider themselves chosen identify themselves with a God who selects and rejects, and so they too select and reject others. In this process, they also become fearsome in the eyes of those they reject.

However, what happens when other groups and other peoples also act in accordance with similar inner images? The result is clear in religious wars. Such groups are neither aware of themselves nor of any others as individual persons. Both sides behave as if possessed by a collective madness.

But in the Christian soul, there is an additional factor: Christians believe in the same God as Jews. So, Christians, in the name of the God of the Jews, see the Jewish people as rejected and robbed of their rights by this common God. The terrible dimensions such a presumption can assume was demonstrated in our time by the Nazi attempt to destroy the Jewish people as a whole.

One might raise the objection here that the Nazi leaders and the Nazi movement were not Christian in any sense of the word. We must not allow ourselves to be blinded on this point, because the Nazi sense of being chosen reflected an essentially Christian characteristic. The "Führer" felt called by providence to lead the new chosen people – in this case a supposedly superior race – to world dominance and, along the way, to eliminate the previous chosen people. As distorted and blind as this may seem to us now, National Socialism, together with a large portion of the German people, drew energy for the Second World War primarily from this sense of mission. The atrocities at their hands were essentially performed in the service of a godly judgement.

This sense of mission was not overcome with the collapse of the Third Reich. We see it even now in the movements of left and right wing radicals. These movements demonstrate a similar sense of mission, and as a consequence, often a blind readiness to use violence against others.

## JESUS, THE CHRIST

The opposition of the old and new chosen people cannot alone explain the aversion of many Christians to the Jewish people, nor the cruelty of the pogroms and deportations. There is yet another root that seems to me to be the most important of all. This has to do with the irreconcilable difference between Jesus, the man of Nazareth, and the belief in his resurrection and ascension to the right hand of God.

For the early Christians, Jesus as a man quickly faded into the background. The image of the ascended Christ was imposed on Jesus the man until he dimmed and became unrecognizable. This allows Christians to repress the painful reality that Jesus on the cross felt abandoned by God, that the God in which he had believed did not appear.

Eli Wiesel, the noted Jewish author, reports a public hanging of a child in a concentration camp. Looking at this atrocity, someone asked, "Where is God, here?" Eli Wiesel answered, "That's him hanging there."

As Jesus on the cross cried out loudly, "My God, my God, why hast Thou forsaken me?" someone might also have asked, "Where is God here?" The answer would have been the same, "That's him hanging there."

The disciples could not bear the reality of their Jesus abandoned by his God. They fled from it through the belief in his resurrection and through the belief in Jesus as the Christ sitting at the right hand of God, and in his second coming to judge the living and the dead. And yet, the man, Jesus, and his human fate, have not been erased by this belief in the resurrection. It lives on in the image of the Jew. Judaism, in the soul of Christians, primarily represents Jesus the man, whom the Christian, believing in the resurrection from the dead and ascendance to the right hand of the Father, dares not see. Christians are afraid to face their God-forsaken Jesus, and their fear makes them nasty. So, just as they turn away from Jesus the man, so do they turn against the Jews as a manifestation of the Jesus they fear, and against the God of Jesus and the Jews, whom they also fear. This is the picture I get when I look at what happens in the souls of many Christians. I'll give you an example:

An incident occurred during a course in group dynamics for very active Christians. The participants were all theologians and served in high positions in their respective churches. The group leader suggested putting an empty chair in the middle of the group, and the group members were to imagine Jesus sitting on this chair. Each person could say something to him. One participant immediately put a chair in the centre and the others began to speak to Jesus. The hatred towards Jesus erupting from the speakers was unbelievable. At one point, a participant even ran into the kitchen to get a knife, with which he then stabbed the chair. When it was over, everyone was stunned at what had come up from the depths of their soul, and they felt terribly ashamed. The group leader, who had been deemed non-

Christian by these dedicated Christians, said, "I find no guilt in this man."

If I picture Jews during their persecution in the Third Reich, and allow this image to work in me, I see them being herded together and sent to their death. I imagine them complying without resistance, gentle and humble, and I see Jesus in them. Jesus the man; Jesus the Jew. The victims of the Holocaust were in a role conspicuously like the Christian Jesus facing the Jews. As a people, and in their behaviour, and in their fate, they embodied the behaviour and the fate of the Christian Jesus facing the Councillors and Pilot. This time, the Christians were the brutes and the Jews exemplified the characteristics of Jesus.

## THE SAME GOD

To return to the idea of God's "choosing", I would like to say something about the beginnings of religion in the soul, and about what happens in the souls of Christians when they become Christians, and in the souls of Jews when they become Jews.

A child is born into a particular family, has particular parents, within a particular extended family. The child has a particular culture, is part of a particular people, and a particular religion. The child cannot choose any of these things.

If the child takes this life as it comes to him or her, without qualifications, if the child takes this life, with everything included in this family – the family fate, the possibilities, the limits; the joy and the suffering – then the child is open, not only to these parents, not only to this people, not only to this particular culture, not only to this particular religion; this child is open to God, and to whatever it is that we may sense beyond this name. Taking life in this way is a religious act, it is *the* religious act.

Someone born into a Jewish family cannot do anything else, and *may* not do anything else except to begin the path to God in a Jewish way. It is the only possible way open to this person, and, therefore, the only right way. The same is true for a Christian on the Christian path. Whatever the differences in beliefs between Christians and Jews, they are the same when it comes to this essential religious act. This movement is independent of the contents of their religions and cannot and may not ever be relinquished, even should the person adopt a different religion later. I'll give you an example.

16

There was once a young man on a course who was looking for help because he felt cut off from life. It emerged that his grandfather had been born a Jew, but this young man considered himself Christian, not Jewish. When we set up a constellation of his family, I put in five representatives next to his grandfather to represent victims of the Holocaust. The grandfather's representative spontaneously laid his head on the shoulder of the representative nearest him. After a while, he said, "This is my place". When the young man was asked to say to his grandfather, "I am also a Jew, and I remain a Jew", he could only manage to say it with great anxiety and trembling. However, once he was able to say that, he felt his own weight for the first time in his life.

What was truly religious in this case? His identification with Christianity or his return to his Jewish roots? The most basic religious act was his acknowledgement, "I am a Jew and I remain a Jew."

A tree cannot choose the place it grows. Yet the place where its seed fell to earth is the right place for that tree. The same thing is true for us. The place where the parents are is the only possible place for each human being, and, therefore, the right place. Each person belongs to a people, has a language, a race, a religion, and a culture which are the only ones possible, and therefore, the right ones. When an individual agrees in the deepest sense to humbly take this from that which is greater than all individuals, and when the individual then develops appropriately, given whatever is possible, then he or she feels equal to everyone else. At the same time comes the recognition that this superior force, whatever we choose to call it, must look at us all as the same. No matter how different the peoples of the world may be, they are all the same before this greatness.

## GERMANS AND JEWS

Given this background, one has to ask, "How can Christians, above all the Germans, handle their guilt towards the Jews? What can they do and what must they do, to overcome this guilt and give the Jewish people a worthy place within themselves? And, how can the Jewish people handle the guilt of Christians and Germans?"

I have had experiences in various courses that indicate how a reconciliation may be possible between victims and perpetrators, and, in a larger sense, between Germans and Jews. One of the most dramatic was an experience during a course in Bern. A man set up a constellation of his present family, and then at the end he said he had to add something important – he was Jewish. I responded by setting up seven representatives of Holocaust victims, and behind them, seven representatives for the dead perpetrators. I asked the seven victims' representatives to turn and look into the eyes of the perpetrators. After that, I did nothing more. I left their movements entirely up to them as they developed.

Some of the perpetrators collapsed, writhing on the floor and sobbing loudly in pain and shame. The victims turned to the perpetrators and looked at them. They helped those who were on the floor to get up, held them in their arms, and comforted them. Finally, an indescribable love emerged between them. One of the perpetrators was completely rigid and could not move in any way. I put in another person to represent the perpetrator behind the perpetrator. The first representative leaned back against this new representative and was able to relax somewhat. The man said later that he had felt like a finger on a giant hand, totally at its mercy. This was also reported by the others in this constellation. All of them, victims as well as perpetrators, felt directed but also carried by some greater force, a force whose effects were not clear.

After this constellation, I asked all the participants to send me a report of what they had experienced during the constellation. One representative of a perpetrator wrote to me:

"As you placed the seven of us behind the seven victims, I was overcome by a very strange, unpleasant feeling. I intuitively anticipated something bad, even though it wasn't yet clear to me at that time who we were representing. When you said that we were the perpetrators a cold chill ran up my spine. When the victims turned and I looked at the man opposite me, all the energy drained out of my body. I have never felt such shame in my life. I just looked at him and kept getting smaller as he kept getting bigger. I wanted nothing more than to disappear into a hole in the ground, preferably a mouse hole deep under the earth. Inside I was screaming "NO! NO! NO! This can't be true." I felt a need to apologize, but at the same time an inner voice told me that there was no way to apologize, nothing could be glossed over, I had to carry it all myself. The only word that I managed to get out was "please", at which point my victim took me in his arms. Without his support I would have fallen to the floor in shame. In his arms, my inner voice kept saying, "I don't deserve this, I don't deserve this at all, to be held by him." Luckily, I was able to let my tears flow otherwise the whole thing would have been unbearable. After my victim had let me go again, I felt somewhat better. I could vaguely feel the floor beneath my feet and could breathe a bit more freely. At the same time I was aware that he was only the first victim, and there were still many more victims on my conscience. Not just two or three – no, dozens or even hundreds! I felt a strong need to look each of these victims in the eye, and so to find my own inner peace.

"As you put the super-perpetrator behind us, it was immediately clear to me that I alone had to carry the responsibility for everything I had done. There wouldn't be any relief from this perpetrator in the background. I also felt very strongly that it would have been much better to have been standing on the other side and not to have taken on this insane guilt.

"My need to look at the next victim got more intense, but in fact, the next eye contact literally threw me to the ground. I couldn't stand up any more and I wept bitterly on the floor. I was totally gone. I was only aware of your faraway voice saying, "Now come slowly back" at a great distance, and the coming back was very slow. There was still too much left undone for me; too many victims not looked at. There was still a powerful urge to bring order into this unfinished business.

"After the constellation it took me at least an hour to get fully back into myself again and to feel my full strength."

"For me, it was truly one of the most difficult roles I've ever experienced in a family constellation. It was also strange how crystal clear thoughts emerged in my awareness. For example, that it is impossible to push the responsibility for your own actions off onto someone else, even if you were only a small cog in the machine. After such an experience, you know there is nothing more to discuss, to argue about, or to explain. It simply is how it is."

In a constellation like this, it also becomes clear that there are no groups, in the sense of one group of victims and another of perpetrators. There are only the individual victims and individual perpetrators. Each individual perpetrator must face the individual victims and each individual victim must face the individual perpetrators.

What becomes clear is that there is no peace for the dead victims until the dead perpetrators have taken their place next to them – until the dead perpetrators have been taken into the souls of their victims. And, there is no peace for the perpetrators until they have lain next to their victims as equals.

If this does not take place, if it is not allowed to happen, the perpetrators will be represented by someone in a later generation. For example, as long as the perpetrators from the last war are denied a place in the souls of the Germans, they will be represented by right wing radicals. In constellations of Jewish families where there are descendants of victims of the Holocaust, I have often seen a child identified with one of those perpetrators. There is no real alternative to a reconciliation, even with the perpetrators.

In these constellations, it is also clear that entanglements are only resolved between those who are actually affected, that is, between a specific perpetrator and a specific victim. No one else can step in on their behalf, no one else has the right, the task, or the power to do so. In the constellations, the representatives of the dead victims and the dead perpetrators do not want the living interfering in their affairs. They want the living to stay out of things and they want life to go on, without being limited or burdened by memories of them. From the viewpoint of these representatives of dead people, life belongs to the living, who are free to take it.

I have a fantasy about this in terms of what effect it would have on the souls of Christians if they were to imagine Jesus dead, meeting in the realm of the dead all those who betrayed him, judged him, and executed him. When we look at them as human beings, also equal in the face of the greater powers that control their destinies, then we have to give them our respect, although this may be a repellent thought for many of us. Above all, we have to honour and respect the greater power behind them and behind us all as a fathomless mystery. To submit to this mystery in this way – that is something truly religious and human.

I once did an exercise with a Jewish woman in whose family many had been murdered. She felt called upon to reconcile the living and the dead. I had her close her eyes and go in her imagination into the realm of the dead. She stood among the six million victims of the Holocaust and looked forwards, backwards, to the left, and to the right. Around the edge of this mass of six million dead lay the dead perpetrators. Then, they all stood up, the dead victims and the dead perpetrators, and all turned towards the horizon to the east. There they saw a white light and they all bowed down before this light. The woman also bowed down with all the dead, and when she was finished she withdrew slowly, leaving the dead in memory before that which appeared on the horizon, but yet remained hidden. Then she turned from the dead and faced life again.

## RECOMPENSE

Sometimes, the living need to face the dead, to look at them and be looked at by them – primarily, those who bear some guilt in respect to the dead, but also those who have gained some advantage from the terrible fate of their Jewish neighbours. In many constellations, what has emerged is that those individuals who had been wronged affected the individual souls of those who had wronged them, or the souls of those who had benefited from those wrongs, and the souls of their descendants as well. This influence continued until the wrong was acknowledged and faced, until the victim was acknowledged as a person of equal value, respected, and mourned. When this was done, the cleft could be sealed, and the terrible effects of the wrongs ceased.

In conclusion, I will tell you a story that will take you on a journey of the soul should you wish to come along.

### The Turning Point

*A man was born into his family, into his homeland, into his culture. Even as a child he was told of the teacher and master whose example was to be followed, and he felt a deep yearning to follow this man and become like him.*

*He joined others who thought the same way and practised a strict discipline for many years, following this example, until he became like the master, and thought and spoke and felt and desired just as the master.*

*Still, he felt something was missing. So he set out on a long journey, to seek the loneliest places and perhaps cross the ultimate boundary. He passed by an old garden, long since abandoned, where only wild roses still bloomed, and where fruit from the huge trees fell unnoticed to the ground because there was no one who wanted it. On the other side of this garden began the desert.*

Soon he was surrounded by an unknown emptiness. It seemed to him that every direction was the same, and the images that sometimes appeared before him also proved to be empty. He roamed on as he felt driven, and when he had long since given up trusting his senses, he saw a spring in front of him. It bubbled out of the earth and the water soaked quickly back into the soil. As far as the water reached, however, the desert was transformed into a paradise.

As he looked around, he saw two strangers approaching. They had done just as he himself had done, and had followed the example of their master until they were like him. They too had been on a long journey through the loneliness of the desert in hope of crossing the final boundary. They had found, as he had, the spring. Together they bent down to drink of the same water, and each believed himself to be almost at his goal. They said their names: "I have become Gautama, the Buddha." – "I have become Jesus, the Christ." – "I have become Mohammed, the Prophet."

The night descended and above them, just as before, shone the stars, still unreachably remote and still. They were all silent, and one of the three knew he was closer to his master than ever before. It was as if he had a sense, for an instant, of how it had been for him as he had known helplessness, futility, and humility. And how he must have felt, too, as he knew guilt.

The next morning he turned back and escaped out of the desert. Once again he passed by the abandoned garden and continued until he came to the garden that was his own. At his gate stood an old man, as if he had been waiting for him. The old man spoke. "One who has found his way back from such a distance as you loves the moist earth. He knows that all that grows also dies, and when it is finished, it nourishes." The man answered, "Yes. I agree to the laws of the Earth." And he began to husband his garden.

# Complete and Incomplete Dying *

HELLINGER *to group* This morning I read an article that had to do with the reciprocal dependency of life and death. The writer's observations were that people who kill themselves or who die suddenly, for example in war or the aftermath, often do not seem to die completely. They do not seem to separate fully from the living, but stay bound to those who are still alive, having a disruptive effect in their lives.

I'll give you an example: Earlier, a man told me that he felt unloved, and that his father and grandfather had also felt this way. In looking for a resolution that could be useful in this case, I was reminded of the work of a friend of mine that had proved to be very effective. He recognized that those who have died suddenly or violently need to turn away from the living and turn to those who have died previously. I had an image that it would be helpful for this man who felt so unloved to lie next to his deceased father. The father would then turn away from his son and turn in the direction of his own dead father. In this way, instead of orientating himself to the living, he would be turning to those who had died before him. Then there can be a parting from the living and the dead man moves in the direction of the realm of the dead.

This may sound peculiar to some of you, but constellations provide access to such pictures and the soul can feel whether it's helpful or not. Of course, you can't simply take this as given and apply it. Every soul needs to find its own individual way. Nonetheless, it was noticeable as I observed the group here how many participants seemed to feel an inner accord with what I described.

* Course in Bern, Switzerland

......

# Jonas*
# The Dead

## COMMENT

This constellation occurred during a course for couples, and began with the search for a solution to a relationship problem. In the course of the work, Jonas also revealed that he was Jewish.

## SUMMARY

The entanglements: *Jonas has repeatedly indicated his desire to end his life. This is threatening to his wife and child. When his father and grandfather stand behind him in the constellation, he feels strong enough to remain in his life. When he mentions that he is Jewish and that his sister had committed suicide, it seems clear that he is involved in the Jewish fate, even though no one in his family was killed.*

The resolution: *Seven people are chosen to represent victims of the Holocaust. They are placed in the constellation in front of Jonas and his family. Jonas approaches them and embraces each one individually. Seven more people are placed behind the victims, to represent their murderers. The victims turn to face them, and a movement of reconciliation begins between them. In the end, they all feel subject to a larger, less personal force, and can meet in love in the face of this greater movement. The dead reject the attempts of the living to interfere in this matter. Jonas and his family pull back from the dead with a feeling of freedom.*

HELLINGER *to Jonas and Brigitte*  What's the issue?

* Course in Bern, Switzerland

JONAS  I'm very satisfied with our relationship, but I think my problem is that I bring too little into the relationship, so my wife would be justified in feeling dissatisfied with me.

BRIGITTE  That's his fantasy. We've been married for seven years and have a six-year-old daughter. When we got married, my husband had a problem with a ringing in his ears. He declared that if it didn't stop he didn't want to go on living. Then, two years ago, he had a knee operation and instead of taking pain medication he took sleeping tablets. That led to a sleep disturbance to the point that he couldn't sleep anymore, naturally with all the accompanying difficulties that brings. At that time he again said he wanted to die if the problem didn't get better. He often says that. He often says that if he didn't have us he would be gone.

HELLINGER  That's very threatening for others.

*To Brigitte*  How old are you?

BRIGITTE  47.

HELLINGER *to Jonas*  How old are you?

JONAS  62

HELLINGER  At 62 one does begin to orientate somewhat towards the end.

JONAS  Yes. But I have to say that I'm doing better now, in large part due to Brigitte and our daughter. I got over the addiction to sleeping tablets with the help of a professor in Bern. Now I'm doing well.

HELLINGER *to group*  This is actually not a relationship problem, but rather Jonas's personal problem.

*To Jonas*  Have you been married before?

JONAS  I wasn't ever married. I had many relationships, but none were steady. There was one abortion.

BRIGITTE  He was also married once, briefly.

*To Jonas*  Were there any children from this marriage?

JONAS  No children.

*To Brigitte*  Have you been married previously?

BRIGITTE  Yes, and I have a 21-year-old daughter from that marriage.

*To Jonas*  What about your family of origin?

JONAS  In my family of origin …

HELLINGER  I'll just take you and your mother in the constellation.

*Jonas chooses representatives for himself and his mother and places them in relationship to each other.*

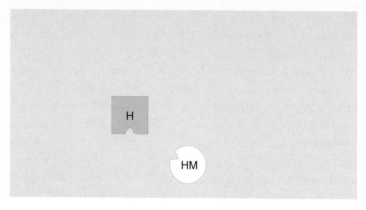

**H    Husband (Jonas)**
HM   Husband's mother

*As the representatives are placed, the mother's representative is looking lovingly at Jonas's representative whereas he is looking away from the mother, to the right and down. After a while he turns to look at the mother. After a pause, Hellinger goes to him and turns him back to the right.*

HELLINGER *to Jonas*  When your representative looks to the right, he looks down. Who or what is he looking at?
JONAS  At his dead father.
HELLINGER  How old were you when he died?
JONAS  I was 17, but I was very immature.
HELLINGER  How did he die?
JONAS  He died suddenly of a stroke.

*Hellinger chooses a representative for Jonas's father and has him lie on his back on the floor, directly in Jonas's representative's line of vision. The representative turns to the dead father, then kneels down to look at him.*

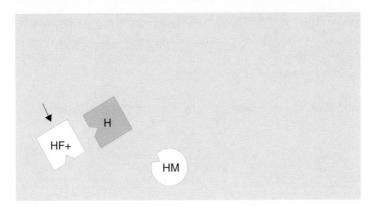

HF   Husband's father+ (died suddenly when Jonas was 17 years old)

HELLINGER *to father's representative* Close your eyes and lie still like a dead person.

*Jonas's representative sits back on his heels and stares at the father unceasingly. The mother's representative moves slowly closer.*

HELLINGER *after a while, to mother's representative* Take him by the hand, stand together, and move away slowly.

*The mother and son move backwards slowly. In the meantime they look at each other, and then turn to one another. The mother holds the son's arm. Then, they both look at the dead man again.*

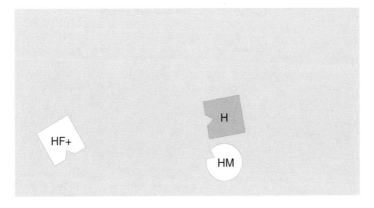

HELLINGER *after a while, to Jonas's representative* What's going on?

27

Husband  The mother is somehow demanding. I don't know where I belong. She seems to take charge of me. I don't know if I want to be that close to her.

Hellinger *to mother*  Let go of him.

*Hellinger leads Jonas's representative some distance away from the mother.*

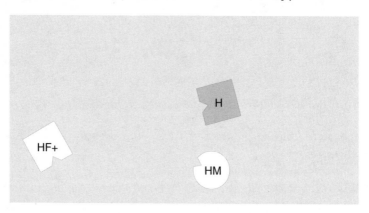

Husband  Actually, I'd rather go closer to the father again.

Hellinger  Stay as you are.

*Hellinger chooses a representative for the father's father and has him lie on his back to the left of Jonas's father.*

Hellinger *to grandfather*  Look over at your father.

*Jonas's representative turns and moves slightly away.*

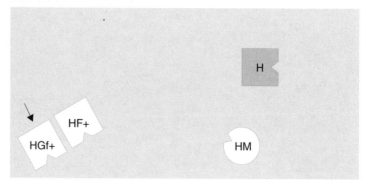

HGf    Husband's Grandfather+

28

*After a while, Hellinger places representatives for Jonas's wife and daughter in the constellation.*

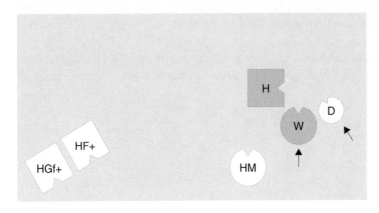

W    Wife (Brigitte)
D    Daughter

*The three look at each other for a long time. Then, Hellinger moves the wife to the other side of her husband. He first looks down at the floor, and then turns slightly towards the wife.*

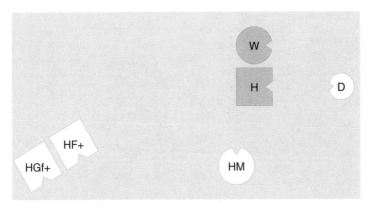

HELLINGER *to father* How are you doing?

HUSBAND'S FATHER I'm feeling just fine. At first, when I lay down, I was very angry. That alternated with a feeling of grief, of not being able to do anything more, of having been struck down. Then something happened and I felt calmer and more at peace. Now that my dead father is here, it's really good. To my right everything has been cut off, and to my left there's a new connection and energy.

HELLINGER *to grandfather* And you?

HUSBAND'S GRANDFATHER I'm doing well. It's very nice to have a son.

*Hellinger moves the father and the grandfather behind Jonas's representative. They each lay their hands on the shoulders of the man in front of them.*

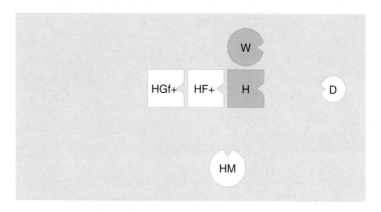

*After a while, Hellinger moves the daughter in front of Jonas's representative. They embrace warmly.*

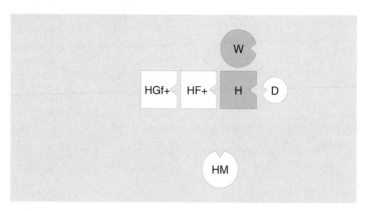

HELLINGER *after a while, to Jonas* How are you doing?

JONAS Could I say something?

HELLINGER Look at this.

JONAS It's exactly right. It's even stronger perhaps because I'm a Jew. Although our family didn't come to any actual physical harm during the Second World War, my willingness to die is strengthened by that. This constellation is exactly as things are.

BRIGITTE His mother's sister committed suicide because she couldn't stand having survived.

HELLINGER That's yet another aspect to be considered, and I'll address that as well.

*To Jonas* Take your place in the constellation.

*As Jonas takes his place, he and the wife and child spontaneously embrace each other very warmly.*

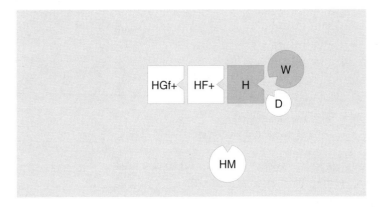

HELLINGER *to Jonas's representative* How was that for you in the constellation?

HUSBAND'S REPRESENTATIVE The most astonishing thing was with my ears. I had an enormous pressure in my ears. When the father and grandfather stood behind me, I could contemplate a human relationship. Before that it wasn't actually thinkable.

*Hellinger chooses seven representatives for Jewish victims of the Holocaust. He places them opposite Jonas.*

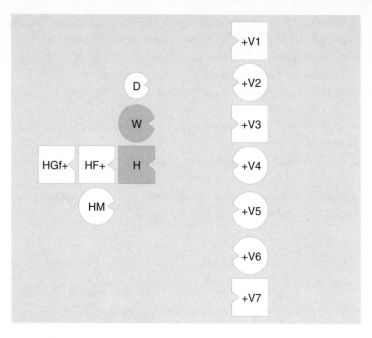

+V1   First murdered victim
+V2   Second murdered victim, etc.

HELLINGER *to Jonas* Do you know who they are?
JONAS I imagine they are the dead.
HELLINGER Exactly.

*Hellinger moves Jonas next to the dead and has him look at them. Then he asks Jonas to go to each of the representatives of the dead and embrace each one. Jonas goes to each and embraces them. Hellinger tells him to breathe deeply as he does this. Meanwhile, Hellinger chooses seven representatives for the deceased perpetrators and places them behind their victims. When Jonas has finished embracing the dead, he returns to his place next to his wife.*

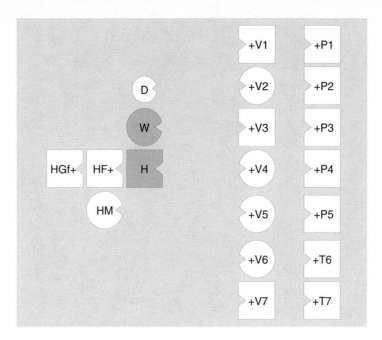

+P1 First Perpetrator
+P2 Second Perpetrator, etc.

HELLINGER *to Jonas* How is that?

JONAS I feel thankful and I want to live.

*To the dead* I'm certain that you understand.

HELLINGER The perpetrators are standing behind the victims.

*To the murdered victims* Turn around and look at the perpetrators.

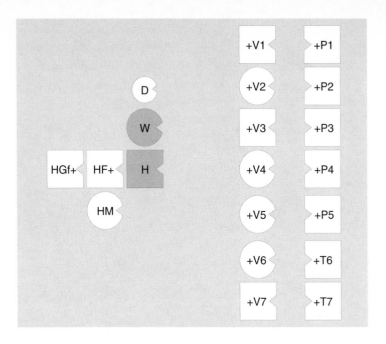

It takes a while before the perpetrators and the victims can meet each other face to face. Then a movement begins. First they come closer together, and then finally, they touch foreheads. The second perpetrator, looking down, holds out his hand to the second victim. After a while they embrace. The fifth perpetrator bows deeply and he and the fifth victim hold hands, looking at the floor. They embrace and then release and look at each other. After a long look, they embrace again. The first perpetrator is very moved and the first victim goes to him. The perpetrator embraces the victim and, sobbing, lays his head on the victim's shoulder. The victim holds him and after a while they look at one another.

The second perpetrator moves closer to his victim and they embrace, but for a long time the perpetrator is not able to look at his victim. Finally, they make eye contact.

In the meantime, the seventh perpetrator and victim look at each other, and the perpetrator puts his hand on his heart and bows. Then, he is held by his victim and lays his head on his victim's breast. After a long time, they are able to look at each other directly and embrace.

It takes a long time before the fourth victim and perpetrator can make contact. The perpetrator turns away from his victim repeatedly, but each time turns back to face him again.

*The third victim and perpetrator remain motionless for a long time. The perpetrator seems as hard as a rock. After a long time, the victim moves to him, but the perpetrator remains unmoved. Hellinger puts another representative behind this perpetrator to represent the perpetrator behind the perpetrators.*

*During this process, Jonas stares down at the floor for a long time. Hellinger asks him to turn to his father. Jonas lays his head on his father's shoulder and they embrace. Jonas's mother joins the embrace after a while. Later, Hellinger asks Jonas to turn and breathe deeply while watching the encounter of the victims and perpetrators. Hellinger then moves Jonas's daughter in front of her father with her back to him. He lays his hands on her shoulders.*

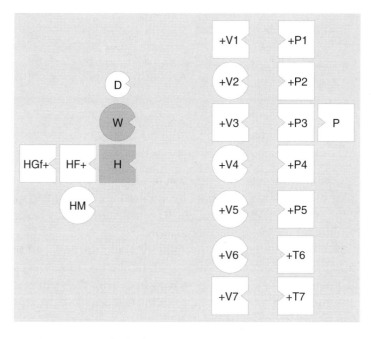

P     Perpetrator in the background

*The third perpetrator rests his head on the perpetrator behind him, but remains unmoving and rigid. He closes his eyes.*

*After a while, the first victim and his perpetrator, who is leaning against him, turn towards the living. The others follow suit, with the exception of the third and fourth pair. The victims and perpetrators stand close together in pairs, or with the perpetrators standing behind their victims, holding* them.

*This meeting of victims and perpetrators takes about 15 minutes and takes place completely in silence.*

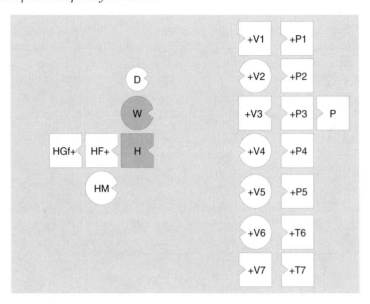

HELLINGER *to first victim* How are you feeling?

FIRST VICTIM I'm doing well, but I have a need for the living to move away from us into their own sphere. It bothers me that they're standing so close to us. We're fine on our own.

FIRST PERPETRATOR *(crying)* It's terrible. He's only the first, and there are hundreds in front of me. The perpetrator behind us has no effect at all. It would have been easier to have been with the victims from the beginning. *He stands next to his victim and, after a while, lays his head on his victim's shoulder and cries.*

SECOND PERPETRATOR I'm standing up, but inside I'm falling down. At first I felt so ashamed I couldn't look at my victim. Now, though, we're one. We have a very deep connection.

SECOND VICTIM I have the feeling that there's no difference between us. I feel very secure.

HELLINGER *to fifth victim* And you?

FIFTH VICTIM *(leaning backwards against his perpetrator)* I feel peaceful and I feel love for him.

FIFTH PERPETRATOR For a long time it felt very free and peaceful. When the perpetrator came in behind us, I felt nervous again. I also wish the living would have nothing more to do with us.

SIXTH VICTIM *(also leaning against his perpetrator)* I'm not yet free of him (Jonas). When he embraced me, his hands felt like claws holding on to me. I'm fine with the perpetrator. Our contact was very moving.

HELLINGER *to Jonas and the others with him* Move a bit further away. Move very slowly backwards.

*They move about eight meters backwards. Hellinger has them all turn sideways away from the dead.*

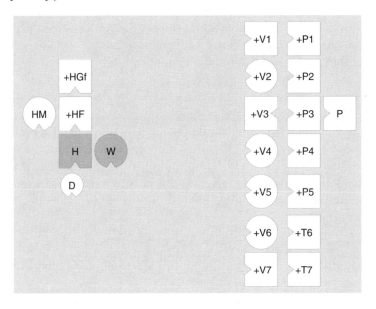

HELLINGER *to sixth perpetrator* How was that for you?

SIXTH PERPETRATOR I had no feelings at all. I would have to bow down to hundreds of victims before anything else would be possible. Totally untouched.

SEVENTH VICTIM *(leaning against his perpetrator)* His embrace (Jonas's) was too brief.

The perpetrator has to hold me. I wanted to say that to him. I feel as if I'm holding the perpetrator and that's why I can't stand.

SEVENTH PERPETRATOR I felt like everything had to come from the victim. I was so full of shame that I wasn't allowed to take the first step.

I felt very thankful that he came to me. I can feel that we're somehow connected to each other.

HELLINGER *to fourth victim* And you?

FOURTH VICTIM I slowly surrendered to my death and to my love for my perpetrator.

FOURTH PERPETRATOR My victim's love released me. That was astounding, what came from her.

HELLINGER *to third victim* And for you?

THIRD VICTIM *(standing opposite his perpetrator)* I suddenly felt that I couldn't reach this perpetrator with love. Then I felt more like an avenging angel and that felt good. When the second perpetrator came in behind him we were more able to make contact with each other. I couldn't let go. At the moment there's a connection between us, but we're not at the point where he can get past his guilt. I'd like to forgive him, but I can't really reach him.

HELLINGER *to third perpetrator* And you?

THIRD PERPETRATOR I was like stone from the very beginning. I had no feelings, no excitement, and no movement. I won't allow it. It simply isn't possible. There's an extremely powerful force holding me. It comes from deep down beneath my feet and is also connected with him (the perpetrator in the background). When he came in, it was the first time that any contact at all was possible with the victim, but I still have no feelings. I like the victim as avenging angel the best. That's right.

THIRD VICTIM I noticed that.

HELLINGER *to third victim* You have to refuse him that.

THIRD VICTIM Yes, I will. I just have to get a ground to stand on, then it'll be okay again.

HELLINGER *to perpetrator in the background* How about you?

PERPETRATOR IN THE BACKGROUND At first my position was very clear but I couldn't feel anything. I was using both of them, victim and perpetrator. Now that some emotion is beginning to stir, I don't feel so sure of myself. I notice that there's an immeasurable guilt there.

HELLINGER *to Jonas* How are you feeling now?

JONAS I feel more solid. I would like to thank everyone.

*To all the representatives and participants* Thank you.

HELLINGER *to Brigitte's representative* How are you?

WIFE I feel very stiff.

HELLINGER It's a huge thing here that you're taking on.

*Hellinger moves her next to her daughter.*

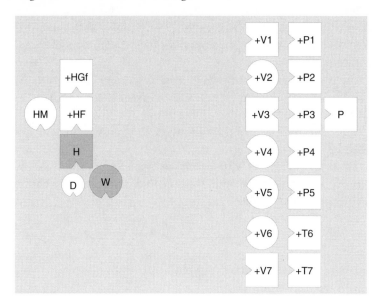

HELLINGER How is that now?

WIFE That's better.

HELLINGER *to daughter* And you?

DAUGHTER I feel fine here. Before, the burden was almost too much. My father was supporting himself on my shoulders. When we moved backwards, it was much lighter up here. I feel good in this place.

HELLINGER How about Jonas's father?

FATHER I feel good here. Earlier, when we were standing over there and the dead Jews came in, they gave off strength. As one of the dead, I first felt a blaming that it could have happened. Then, I felt relieved of that. Bit by bit it let go. It was also very important to me, when my son couldn't confront that, to pull him up and tell him to look at it. I wanted to tell him to look squarely at the truth and then he'd be able to handle it.

HELLINGER *to Jonas's grandfather* What about you?

GRANDFATHER I feel good here. What I noticed was that when I looked at the people, I couldn't be with the family anymore, or take care of them. I felt a need to look away and look at my children. Otherwise that wasn't possible.

HELLINGER And Jonas's mother?

MOTHER  At first I felt paralyzed and could only look at my son. As my husband lay on the floor, I could only think how I didn't want to lose my son, too. I was thinking, "Hold on." It was all the same to me when the victims and perpetrators came in. I was still thinking, "Hold on until it's over."

FATHER  It's interesting, but I haven't really got any connection to my wife. My son is very important, and the need to give him strength and support.

MOTHER  I'm more or less reaching with one hand to his father, and one to my son.

HELLINGER *to Jonas* I want to tell you something important about a situation like this. When the dead see that a survivor has children, they're comforted. Right?

*Jonas nods affirmation.*

HELLINGER  That's important for you.

JONAS  Yes, that's true.

HELLINGER  Now your face is lighting up. Good. That's what was missing.

*In the meantime, the movement between the victims and perpetrators has continued. Some have sunk to the floor. The seventh victim has seated himself in front of his murderer, leaning back against him.*

HELLINGER *to Jonas and his family, as he sees this* This group can sit now. The other one isn't finished yet. Just remain removed from the group of victims and perpetrators so you don't disturb their dynamic.

*After a while to the representatives of the victims and perpetrators* Slowly come out of your roles now. Make your connections again to your own centre and your own forefathers and leave these feelings here.

*To representative of the first perpetrator* Thank God you're Swiss! *Laughter in the group.* Okay? Are you getting out of this?

*To all representatives of the victims and perpetrators* Thank you all for taking on these difficult roles.

REPRESENTATIVE OF THE FIRST PERPETRATOR  I had the image of hundreds of victims standing in front of me whom I would have to contact individually in this way. I can't deal with it as a package deal, I've got to do it one by one. As I turned to the second victim, it was a bit easier, but there's still a lot there.

HELLINGER Thank you for sharing that.

REPRESENTATIVE OF THE FIRST VICTIM It was completely crazy, the longer we stood there, the more I felt like I loved them. The longer we stood there, the more I felt their entanglements and could willingly allow myself to be killed. I agree to that completely because I can see that it's also a resolution for their entanglements. I've never experienced anything like this before.

HELLINGER Okay. Thank you all.

*The representatives all take their seats again.*

HELLINGER *to group* I would like to say something that might help us to understand these connections. It's not enough to look at the victims or to look at the perpetrators, or to look at all of them. The victims and the perpetrators are all embedded in something beyond them.

REPRESENTATIVE OF THE THIRD PERPETRATOR I had the feeling of being like one finger of a giant hand of some huge being. It was totally impersonal.

HELLINGER Exactly. That's a precise image of what I'm talking about. *To group* There must be some force at work that directs the course of history, even in its most terrible aspects. On the one hand that is an awful force, or we could say an awesome force. Huge and absolute. In this force, victims and perpetrators are all the same. That's why the victims and perpetrators are able to love each other when they know themselves to be connected in this greater power. It's only when we acknowledge this and when this religious aspect is brought into the picture (whatever that means in the particulars, and that we can't fathom) that there can be reconciliation and freedom for the living.

# Supplement to Jonas's Constellation: The Dead

When I asked Jonas for permission to include his constellation in a publication, he said it was important to him that I include the following comment: "I was on the side of the victims, but if I had been on the side of the perpetrators I don't believe I would have been any better than the others."

A few days after the seminar, I contacted the representatives of the victims and perpetrators, as well as the representative for Jonas's mother, and asked them to write a short report of their inner experience during the constellation. I include these reports, unedited, in their full length. It should be noted that the representatives are speaking as the dead and refer to processes in the realm of the dead.

## JOHANNES SCHMIDT
### REPRESENTATIVE OF THE FIRST VICTIM

*To begin with, in the constellation there was a heightened awareness that gradually intensified, finally focussing, on the nearness of the SS officer standing closest to me. A deep sense that I had to approach this SS officer, who was clearly agitated. Moving close to this man and taking hold of him firmly, holding him. An odd feeling of closeness and responsibility for this man's soul. I felt his pain and despair clearly and held him to comfort and encourage him. Being close to him was important at that moment, and I felt very grounded and very strong. Eventually, the SS officer freed himself from my embrace. I felt the torture in his soul quite clearly and felt very connected to him and united with him. I kept having a feeling of having to hold him and support him, and there was a deep consent to the terrible events that had happened. I was able to assent to my destiny in every aspect and felt enormously strong. I was standing very firmly on the ground.*

*I suddenly felt an intense compassion for my tormentor's emotional entanglements , and I felt a consent, a willingness, to give my life if that would contribute to untangling these difficulties and to assist his soul. Death didn't have any meaning for me anymore. But this man's progress was important to me, and a kind of love developed. If it's necessary for me to die to assist a development in him and the greater soul, then I'll gladly give my life.*

*Additionally, I very much wished that the living would move away from those events in the realm of the dead. I had an intense urge to lay out some kind of symbol of the separation and boundaries of the living and the dead, to define the realm of the dead and the realm of the living, something like a bunch of roses, for example.*

## CHRISTOF EICKE
## REPRESENTATIVE OF THE FIRST PERPETRATOR

*As you placed the seven of us behind the seven victims, I was overcome by a very strange, unpleasant feeling. I intuitively felt something bad, even though it wasn't yet clear to me who we were representing. When you said that we were the perpetrators a cold chill ran up my spine, and I recognized a confirmation of my first uneasy feelings. When I turned to the victims and looked at the man opposite me, all my energy drained out of my body. I have never felt such shame in my life. I just looked at him and kept getting smaller as he kept getting bigger. I wanted nothing more than to disappear into a hole in the ground, preferably a mouse hole deep into the earth. Inside I was screaming "NO, NO, NO, it can't be. You're big and I'm small." I also felt a need to apologize, but at the same time, an inner voice told me that there was nothing to apologize for, nothing to gloss over, that I had to carry this myself. The only word that I managed to get out was "please," at which point Johannes, as the victim, took me in his arms. Without his support I would have fallen down in shame. In his arms, my inner voice kept saying, "I don't deserve this, I don't deserve this at all, to be held by him." Luckily, my tears could flow, otherwise the whole thing would have been unbearable. After Johannes let me go, I felt somewhat better. I could vaguely feel the floor beneath my feet and could breathe a bit more freely. At the same time I knew that he was only the first victim, and there were still many more victims on my conscience. Not just two or three – no, dozens or even hundreds! I felt a strong need to look each of these victims in the eye, and so to find my own inner peace.*

As you put the super-perpetrator behind us, it was immediately clear to me that I alone had the responsibility to bear everything I had done. There wouldn't be any relief from this perpetrator in the background. I alone could have said no and not acted as a perpetrator. I felt very strongly that it would have been much better to have stood on the other side and not to have taken this insane guilt upon myself.

My need to look at the next victim increased, but in fact, the next eye contact literally threw me to the ground. I couldn't stand up any more and I wept bitterly on the floor. I was totally gone. I was only aware of your faraway voice saying, "Now come slowly back" at a great distance, and the coming back was very slow. There was still too much left undone for me, too many victims not looked at. There was still a strong urge to bring order into this unfinished business.

After the constellation it took me at least an hour to get fully into myself again and to feel my full strength.

For me, it was truly one of the most difficult roles I've ever experienced in a family constellation. It was also strange how crystal clear thoughts emerged in my awareness. For example, that it is impossible to put the responsibility for your own actions onto someone else, even if you were only a small cog in the machine. I'm completely fascinated by these moments in which it's possible to glimpse something of a basic truth. After such an experience, you know there is nothing more to discuss, to argue about, or to explain. It simply is how it is.

## Nico Eichelseder
### Representative of the Second Victim

As I stood facing my perpetrator, I saw a river between us, a large river. It was purely accidental who stood on which side. We both belonged to the same river like two trees growing on opposite banks. My perpetrator and I were as one, taken into service by life; he as perpetrator, and I as victim. I could have just as easily been the perpetrator and vice versa. I recognized him clearly as _my_ perpetrator, as if the perpetrator and victim were a pair that belonged together from the beginning.

At first my feelings were neutral. Then there was a sense of "it" remembering, as though something was coming back from far away. His eyes were gazing at me from far, far away. I felt how I had missed him. As soon as I saw the river between us, it was clear to me how arbitrary our destiny was, almost pure chance which role we got in life.

*I felt a deep sympathy for my perpetrator. I saw the torment in his eyes. His whole being was filled with pain. I didn't feel any hate nor any fear, no aggression, and no memory. What had happened didn't happen <u>between</u> us; we were a piece of the event that "happened to <u>us</u>", and bound us together in a power that took us into its service.*

*My eyes filled with tears. It wasn't a personal grief, but a grief over the helplessness and the fate that forced us to stand facing one another as victim and perpetrator – for a while. It seemed to me that my perpetrator was really the victim. His suffering was perceptible and undiluted.*

*I knew that I had to take the first step and I moved towards him. Slowly my hands reached out to him. It was difficult for him to accept my offering. He began to cry, almost silently, with cautious tears, until they flowed down his cheeks. His eyes began to melt. He took my hands. An eternity passed before we could completely find each other – find each other <u>again</u>, it seemed to me. We took one step towards one another and very slowly our arms opened, around each other, in each other.*

*It was as though we had had a unity long before we became victim and perpetrator. Being victim and perpetrator was an interlude, like something we had to carry. Only at this point, through this reconciliation, were we truly liberated. I felt peace in his arms, almost like an eternal peace. Finally there was peace. I felt so deeply held.*

*We stayed that way a long time, breathing deeply together. It was as if we were drawing breath from a cosmic spring, beyond life, death, and fate. Life and death, perpetrator and victim all seemed like an interlude in the face of this love that had opened up to us. Long, deep breaths. The river that gave birth to us took us back into the arms of its love.*

*Dear Bert, that was such a deep, incomprehensible experience, almost intimate. I trust that you know that I haven't made this up. It was only later, after you had said what you did, that I was aware that I had simply felt that deeply, and that I wasn't crazy. You simply can't imagine that these impressions could be so clear and precise, and so all encompassing. I am thankful that I was allowed to experience this. This is a work of peace between the living and the dead. I know that now.*

## Dirk J. Appel
### Representative of the Second Perpetrator

*As I came up onto the stage and was placed behind the victim, I felt very secure. I stared at the back of the victim. I felt an inner relationship with the row of victims in front of me. I was aware of the other perpetrators, but they weren't important to me. I felt no connection to the descendants of the victim (Jonas's family).*

*When the row of victims turned around, my gaze dropped to the floor. It felt as though every fibre of my body was awash in shame. Every movement I made and every thought I had increased my shame. Although I felt goodwill from the victim facing me, it was impossible for me to move at first, or even to raise my eyes. After a while I was able to look up, drawn by the goodwill of this victim. At the moment our eyes met, tears sprang to my eyes.*

*The victim facing me stretched out her hands to me, but at first my shame was too great to withstand her look, let alone take her hands. I experienced this as too much and not appropriate. I didn't feel worthy of taking her hands, or of taking anything else. At that point it was as if I was standing before a personal threshold of shame.*

*It took a lot of my personal strength to withstand her look and then, finally, to take her outstretched hands. At that point I experienced even more shame, but it didn't feel personal any longer, but rather, impersonal or collective. My whole body felt like one raw wound, and I could only see the victim facing me. It seemed as if I was looking deeper and deeper. The victim's gaze offered something inviting.*

*When I had looked thoroughly, we embraced warmly (the victim and I). At first I held the victim, and through her allowing herself to be held I felt an enormous strength flow through my back. At the point where I couldn't look any deeper, I had the impression that I was sinking deeper and deeper. In this sinking, a kind of love opened up from my heart, and as I sank deeper, there was a kind of "procreative love" and a deep melting there. The strength in my back allowed me to hold the victim with a feeling of never letting go. When that became clear, I had the feeling that we were holding each other.*

*Then, I felt my body standing on the stage, but all feelings of ego-attachment had disappeared. It's difficult, perhaps impossible, to describe this point in words. Even words like deep love seem too shallow. The closest for me would be the words "all-one-being". Everything was present, I was connected to everything, and yet I was gone.*

*First the personal shame left me, then the collective shame, then the love from the heart, then the procreative love, and then, finally, my identity. Then there was only the feeling of "all-one-being", clear presence, and a connection to all the victims, perpetrators, descendants, and the other people there.*

*For me personally, this constellation in Bern was an important, even a spiritual experience.*

## HANS-JOACHIM REINECKE
## REPRESENTATIVE OF THE THIRD VICTIM

*In the constellation I represented a Jewish victim and was placed, along with others, in a row. Opposite us there was a corresponding row of people representing Nazi perpetrators. Following my first impulse, I tried to open my heart to the perpetrator facing me, and to forgive him personally for his misdeeds. I was filled with love and sympathy, but in thinking about it, I wondered if that position was really appropriate and not too presumptuous.*

*To my right and left I was aware of strong exchanges of feelings between the "partners". I was aware that some of the representatives were coming together, and some were embracing, at any rate, making contact. This movement wasn't present between me and my perpetrator. I only felt cold and hard. I opened my arms and tried to help the perpetrator so we could meet, but he didn't show any response. I tried to strengthen my feeling of wanting to forgive, but I sensed that it would require a strength from me which was rapidly disappearing. I started to go weak at the knees, but I continued in my attempts to reach the perpetrator.*

*At the same time, anger was building in me over his unwillingness to reconcile. Although I felt that this feeling was unjustified and presumptuous, the anger grew.*

*By the time I reached the end of my love for the perpetrator, I felt a desire for revenge and a demand for satisfaction. I stared into the perpetrator's eyes and an image came up of a fiery avenging angel with a flaming sword, rather like the depictions in the old illustrated Bibles at the turn of the century. Filled with this image, the energy flowed out through my eyes towards the perpetrator. That was the first time he showed any affect other than seeming cold and unapproachable, as I've already described. He lowered his eyes in uncertainty, and suddenly seemed embarrassed and weaker than before.*

*The effect of my change of attitude was in part the satisfaction I had hoped for, but partly a guilty conscience, because I hadn't really meant to continue the spiral of violence between the unreconciled victim and perpetrator. This conflict within myself weakened me and the perpetrator sensed it. He didn't seem triumphant, although he continued to be rather dominating, but still appeared to be less sure of himself than at the beginning. I didn't notice any sign of regret or anything like that.*

47

When the man facing me was strengthened by the addition of a "superior" behind him, I was aware of a noticeable relief and relaxation in him. Unfortunately, this change didn't have any effect on our relationship. The major effect of the change in the constellation, which was clearly visible to me, was an inner change in the perpetrator facing me.

I was getting noticeably weaker in my helplessness, but in retrospect, the perpetrator didn't allow me even a gesture of forgiveness, and I got weaker at the knees. If the constellation hadn't ended at this point, I would certainly have collapsed. The feeling of weakness, especially at the knees, continued for some hours afterwards.

After the constellation I attempted to filter out the influence of any personal qualities of myself or the man facing me from my experience in the role. In fact, the man in the role of the perpetrator facing me had already come to my attention several times before this constellation. I wanted to sort out to what extent a heightened energy between him and myself earlier in the day could have distorted a personal power struggle between two forces in the constellation. During a break, he and I talked about it but couldn't get any clarification.

## GERHARD WALPER
### REPRESENTATIVE OF THE THIRD PERPETRATOR

You brought us to the stage without any comment and placed us behind the Jewish victims. It was immediately clear to me that I was a perpetrator. I had barely taken my place behind a Jewish man when an unbelievably powerful strength flowed into my body from deep down beneath me. Within a short period of time, I charged up right down to my fingertips. I felt powerful, hard, and impervious to injury with this strength. Nothing could have swayed me from my path, even at the cost of my life. Whatever was happening around me was insignificant to me.

When the Jewish man in front of me turned around, I didn't want to see him and I didn't want to be seen by him. So I looked at his face unwillingly for a long time but without any engagement. This person was meaningless to me. It annoyed me that he looked at me so gently, almost with reconciliation. When he tried to make contact with me and reached out to touch my arm, I hardened completely and became aggressive.

Then, he too looked aggressive and challenging. I thought, "Finally. I can deal with you this way. This is the way I want you." You had him say something like, "I won't make it so easy for you."

48

I waited in this rigidity for a long time and tried to make my opponent give way. When you brought in the perpetrator in the background and stood him behind me, the hardness and tension relaxed for the first time. I leaned back and breathed deeply. Slowly, something that had had me in its grip drained out of me. I returned to a normal human size. I felt tired and heavy and I closed my eyes. My body longed for the ground and for quiet.

When I had returned to my seat, an image came to me. I saw a huge figure and I was a finger on the hand of this being. With no personal identity, no personal will, no personal feelings. My whole experience was somehow anonymous and directed from the outside.

Later I recognized that the Jew in front of me was another part of the same being.

## Michaela Kaden
### Representative of the Fourth Victim

As a representative in the role, I was only aware of the living as if through a veil, without any particular interest or specific feelings. My attention was directed inwards. When the perpetrators were put behind the victims and I sensed that there was a perpetrator behind me, I suddenly felt very interested and, at first, frightened. It was a relief to turn around and look at him. Looking into his eyes, I had a sense of distance and of completeness within myself. I felt myself gaining strength and a very clear, impersonal love. I was calm, with no regrets about what had happened to me and the others, and with no accusations against the perpetrator, without even thinking about that. My tears came, but were less from grief than from being deeply touched and moved by this contact with the other. The other wasn't my enemy; he was foreign to me, but not my enemy. I watched him struggle within himself and I knew that I could only watch him, that I mustn't help. I wasn't allowed to make any move towards him unless he could pull himself up. Holding back, but staying present at the same time cost a lot of my strength and demanded my complete attention. It was compelling, almost like an assigned task.

I was only peripherally aware of the victims and perpetrators to my right and left, and had no particular interest in them. It felt as though we were all pushed by a great movement, but that each was alone in this wave and had his or her own story.

The perpetrator and I began to move slowly and very cautiously towards one another. We touched and laid our heads together. It was gentle, as though this contact was something holy. The more we found our way to-gether, the more I was able to let go of my strength. Although I was still conscious of the distance and clarity, and the feeling of quiet, impersonal love, at the same time I felt that this was becoming personal. At that mo-ment I was struggling with a total surrender to this love. The more the other found his strength and could see me, the less important my own was. As I let myself drop on to his shoulder, I felt a release, like dying in a larger sense, and being at one with a different force. The words in my head were: "I have surrendered to my death and my love." It was like being freed from a duty.

Then it was good to turn around to the living and I felt friendly and supportive and distant from them. From my point of view they couldn't have done anything to lighten my destiny. I had to go on this path with the other who was put opposite me as perpetrator. I needed to stand next to him and look at the living and I knew that he, that we both, were sending out love and no danger for those who were still alive. There was a feeling of dignity and quiet serenity.

### ALBRECHT MAHR
### REPRESENTATIVE OF THE FOURTH PERPETRATOR

When the victim turns around and looks at me, I can't look at her. I can only look down at the floor, feeling a confusing mixture of shame, incomprehen-sion, not understanding, no right to see or be seen. Heavy weeping. I can't move an inch. A longing to be seen by this woman. A brief glance up at her. An uncertain expression in her eyes, but astoundingly enough, goodwill. Continue crying heavily and unable to act. An almost childlike feeling of: she really does want to see me and touch me! No clear sense of guilt or sense of having killed this person. Intense longing for this woman. The longing of a child for love? She touches my hand gently, I scarcely dare to respond. Again, totally unbelievable: goodwill in her eyes! A very cautious taking of hands. She looks so loving. My heart is so moved and opens to the love coming from her and flowing towards her. Uncertain: is this denial, child-ish, avoiding guilt? Finally there is a powerful, even erotic bond of love between us, releasing. I respond to being asked, "Her love has released me." In the end we stand together as one, a loving couple. There's no sense of any awareness of victim and perpetrator.

## Irma Hardmeyer
### Representative of the Fifth Victim

*Bert brings me to the stage in a constellation that has already been going on for some time and that has really captured my interest. As we are moved to our places in the constellation, we're told that we are victims.*

*I feel small, nervous, and lost. To my right and left I sense movement and an unease that isn't visible from the outside. I can't find any place to look, and keep searching for a focus. I finally settle on the "son" (Jonas) and hope he'll see me and know that I'm there.*

*The perpetrators are placed behind us. After a while I feel a great sympathy. I turn around to see who is there. I look at him and try to see the evil in him – something that would surely frighten me. But the longer I look, the more sympathy I feel. I see him, and see his suffering. I see and feel his grief and helplessness. I know that he wasn't able to cope with the situation. My eyes fill with tears and I move cautiously towards him and take him in my arms. I hold him in all his pain. Unbelievably, I notice that a love is developing, a love full of compassion. I speak to him without words, and simply hold him firmly. Slowly we release our embrace and look at each other, we nod to one another and there is peace between us.*

*I see the "super-perpetrator" in the background. Looking at him, something happens that makes me feel very humble and touched. I see an image that is living. (I can't find the words to describe this properly). I see the greater whole, and it's a pulsing of history, a weaving together, a course of events from the beginning to the present. There's no time anymore, only movement.*

*Dazed from what I have seen and experienced, I return to my seat. I have had a glance into being and I can still feel it. It is a release.*


## Christian Müller
### Representative of the Fifth Perpetrator

*As you placed us in the constellation, I thought you wanted to increase the number of victims. I didn't realize at first that I was a perpetrator.*

*As I was placed, I felt very interested in the living, but was clearly aware that we were separated from each other – two groups, from different places. The feeling was similar to what I had felt in the constellation representing a soldier killed in battle.*

*When you said that we were the perpetrators, I was shocked, and as the victims turned around, I was afraid of this confrontation. At first I couldn't* look the victim in front of me in the eye, because I was so ashamed. The victim was big and I was very small. I noticed that she had a kind of power over me, and I felt dependent on her, which was unpleasant on the one hand, but on the other hand was right. I was deeply in her debt, so deeply that I didn't know how or even if anything could happen. The other thing that was bad was that there were so many of us, it wasn't just the two of us. This dimension, of being spread out, was oppressive and made me feel helpless at first.

The victim facing me looked friendly and inviting. I tried to make contact and hold it, but it was difficult and it didn't ring true. Then I felt that a bowing down would be appropriate. It felt right and warm as well to put myself lower than this victim. I didn't bow deeply, just enough so that it felt right.

After that, the relationship with the victim was much more relaxed and open to contact at a different level. I was able to look at her and move towards her. We took each other's hands and then embraced warmly. I felt a very deep connection to this person. I can't describe any exact feelings. It was more like an awareness of a greater entirety, which is a bond, complete, and happy. The events that led to us being victim and perpetrator also belonged to this bond. I could feel that but they weren't "bad" anymore for us directly. On the other hand, I felt grief and pain that it had to be, and that there were similar events to the right and left of me. I was aware that the driving force of evil is much, much larger than all of us.

The bond with the victim was not only very strong, it was existential for me. It was as if the victim had the right to determine whether I could exist or not. Strangely enough, I may have taken this victim's life, and through that, she had my life in her hands.

In any event, I felt respect and gratitude for the greatness of the victim and the way she accepted me. It's a greatness I will never be able to achieve.

At this point, the "perpetrator behind the perpetrators" came into the constellation. This expansion of the system made me very uneasy at first. I was distracted from my relationship with the victim. Just as the group of victims and perpetrators made it clear to me that evil was _everywhere_, the perpetrator in the background made it clear that there had <u>always</u> been evil and always would be. There was a time component and also the aspect of hierarchy. This figure intensified the sense of how enormous this power is, and how small we are. I also noticed, with a feeling of despair, that I stood in a <u>row of perpetrators</u> also in the sense of generations. There were perpetrators before my time, and also after me. There was no way of avoiding this, *even though a reconciliation with the victim was possible. Reconciled or not, we remain perpetrators.*

*As you went on to work with the client's system again, I felt very hopeful. Above all, I tried to send strength to the client himself. He was so rigid and I hoped he would finally soften somewhat.*

*It was important that you turned that system away from us. I was hoping (similar to the other constellation with the dead soldier) that they wouldn't come over to us. I was also hoping that through our reconciliation we could contain and hold some of this evil energy so that the living would have things better. If we can find a reconciliation, then the living are free. On the other hand, we can only find our peace if the living forget about us, at least until they join us. The two realms have to remain separate.*

*It was very difficult to stay with this awareness. I had to keep coming back to the bond to the victim facing me and to myself and our relationship. It would have been easier to give in to what was before, to sink into the mass of the perpetrators, and pass the responsibility on to a higher force. It was only the connection to "my" victim and my consciousness that could pull back the shadow and, I believed that through this effort I could perhaps help the living.*

## BIRGIT HAUSNER
### REPRESENTATIVE OF THE SIXTH VICTIM

*I was brought to the stage as one of the victims in the extermination of the Jews. We are placed in a row facing a man who is also a Jew, but who mostly was unharmed by the assassins. He can't really look at us and Bert encourages him to embrace each one of us. There are five ahead of me and I wait and look forward to my turn. Then it's my turn to be embraced and I feel as if I'm being clutched by claws and I am thunderstruck. After me, there's one more embrace and then he goes back to his place and is able to look at us more easily.*

*Then, Bert brings seven more people up to the stage and places them behind us. After a short while he tells us to turn around as these are the perpetrators.*

*For a moment I felt sick, then I turned around slowly. There is my perpetrator in front of me and I am helpless. I can't look at him very easily because he doesn't want to look at me. I would like to lean on him, to rest on his shoulder, but nothing comes from him. Gradually, I can only stand it if I look down at the floor, and my heavy head bends towards his shoulder.*

There's a struggle between us, and then he allows it to happen and takes my hands. Now it's better. There's no blame, only a simple pain and grief. We hold each other for a while and it quietens down. I still have a burning pain in my upper chest.

Then Bert brings another man who is placed behind all of us. He tells us this is the perpetrator behind the perpetrators. My heart stops again and my emotions run wild. The man is quickly integrated though, and there's an unbelievable heaviness in all this. Then Bert has us turn around to look at the living. I can only stand it when my perpetrator holds his hands on my upper chest (which feels like a sieve, full of holes).

I see another victim fall to the floor, crying, and I feel angry because I can't stand to look at this anymore. I have just enough strength to stay standing. Then Bert ends the constellation.

### GERHARD GÜDEL-ROESTI
### REPRESENTATIVE OF THE SIXTH PERPETRATOR

At first I just felt totally empty. No feelings, no excitement. I didn't know what was supposed to happen, or what I was supposed to do.

All at once, near me, others began to cry or to bow. I couldn't understand what was going on.

Then, I started feeling uncomfortable and wondered why. I was completely helpless and beyond what I could handle, and I didn't know what to do. I felt very lost.

Then I had the urge to do what those next to me were doing, to fit in with the group. I bowed before the woman facing me. As I bowed, I could feel that it was right. I wanted to bow more and more deeply. The bowing down made things easier for me, but I was aware that that wasn't enough. As I straightened up and looked the victim in the eye, I was still completely lost. Gradually a feeling of guilt rose up in me.

At the same time I could also start to feel with the victim and to understand why she looked at me the way she did. When the "perpetrator behind the perpetrators" was brought in, things started to become clearer.

I felt that there was a lot of atonement due before I could find peace. I also felt the importance of my terrible deeds belonging to a larger picture. The only thing that can give me the strength to atone and find peace is the connection to the perpetrators near me and behind me.

I was also aware that a reconciliation with the victim would only be possible when I had made the connection with the other perpetrators.

## STEPHAN HAUSNER
## REPRESENTATIVE OF THE SEVENTH VICTIM

*As I was placed in the constellation, my sympathies were with the client. He had to look at me, the victim, for a long time.*

*When the perpetrators were put behind us, I had chills and was shaking. Then, we turn around and look at the perpetrators. The chills disappear but I'm still trembling. I feel a connection to the perpetrator immediately and can approach him. I can see his pain, which strengthens our connection. I would like to lay my head on his chest, but instead, he moves to me first and lays his head on my chest.*

*It's an uncomfortable sensation, and I'd rather that he had remained standing up straight and let me know in this way that he was taking a stand and would hold me. I need to have his look – that's the only thing that gives me strength. So, I lift up his head so that he looks me in the eye. I understand that this is difficult for him and I feel almost a love for him.*

*The words keep going through my head, "Please, you hold me. It's so hard for me to stand up. I'm so weak, I need you!" (I suddenly have the feeling that although the person facing me is a perpetrator, he doesn't carry a personal guilt. I feel as though I may have died of hunger or weakness in a camp.)*

*I feel a desire for peace and quiet, but I'm aware that I will only come to rest when I have found the perpetrator, so I bear it and keep trying to find a healing contact.*

*After a while we turn around again and at this point I can look at the family with goodwill from a distance. I know that my place is here and their place is there.*

*I would like to lean against the perpetrator, but he moves backwards. I have to sit down and try to lean against him in a sitting position. As he tries to pull away, I hold his legs. I have to be able to feel him. We belong together and I can't exist without him.*


## MARKUS NIEDERHÄUSER
## REPRESENTATIVE OF THE SEVENTH PERPETRATOR

*As Bert placed us on the stage I wasn't yet aware of what role we would be taking. I first thought about the generation before the victims. "You are the perpetrators" came as a shock.*

*I felt incapacitated by the circumstances, that I was responsible for something that couldn't be changed. Incomprehensible! That was me! What had*

I done? And, I can't alter anything. I felt the weight of the suffering I had caused. Feelings of shame and regret. Also a fear of the victim.

When we stood facing one another, I had the feeling that I had no rights, certainly not to take the first step towards the victim. I would need at least some sign, a signal from the victim, in order to approach him. The victim facing me sought contact with me. I felt like looking down, but the victim wouldn't allow any avoidance. After a while, I dared to look him in the eye. That helped. The eye contact was a powerful experience. I felt grateful to him for not pushing me away, but rather allowing me the dignity of contact. A strong feeling that we belong together. A bond ties us together. Closeness, warmth, even love – these made grief possible, and a weeping together over what had happened. In retrospect, I have the feeling that I did too little for the victim – he also felt weak at the knees and said that he hadn't felt supported by me. Because of the confrontation with the incomprehensible, I was very occupied with myself. Danger: to become fully absorbed in the perpetrator role, when the victim could have needed me. As perpetrator, I slid into the role of weakness, the victim.

## Sonja Kriener
### Representative of Jonas's Mother

As the mother I feel an incapacitating burden. I can hardly move my limbs. I feel afraid for my son, an awful fear of something unknown, something terrible. My son is far away from me, kneeling on the floor with his face turned away, and is scarcely reachable. I am afraid of losing him and I reach out searchingly for him with my eyes and try to find him and hold him. I have to go to him. Having made this decision I start moving slowly towards my son. I take him by the hand and pull him up to me, look into his eyes and lead him away. My determined look isn't capable of holding him. I'm not strong enough. There is something powerful that I feel bound to.

As his father, my husband, comes in, I breathe more freely, although I don't feel anything towards my husband. When my husband's father also comes in, the relief is intensified. My son and I hold each other.

I can just look at my son's wife and daughter. My concern is only with my son.

When the victims are placed in front of our little group and I look into their eyes and their familiar faces, there is a deep pain that drives out my stiffness. My entire being, without exception, screams out in pain, but my lips are closed. Only a few tears find the way out.

*As the perpetrators of the victims are added to the constellation I start to feel turbulence – panic – there's no way out. The pain is unbearable, and helplessness so close. I look spellbound at this group, and I'm held up by the love for my son. He is being held by his father and grandfather. When the perpetrator behind the perpetrators comes into the constellation, the deep pain that cannot get any worse leads me through the helplessness. Slowly I begin to feel quieter and calmer. There is a mercy that is having an effect. The circle closes and there is a unity, a great oneness.*

# Edda*
## Child of an SS soldier in the Warsaw Ghetto

### SUMMARY

The entanglements: *Edda's father was with the SS in the Warsaw Ghetto. He was living outside the ghetto with his family when Edda was born. She and her sister were abused by their father. She was previously anorexic, and now has cancer and is bulimic.*

The resolution: *The father is drawn to the victims and has to leave. Otherwise, one of the children will go in his place. Edda says to him, "Dear Papa, even if you go, I'm staying." She stands next to her mother and says, "Papa, I'm staying with my mother. This is my place."*

*From the viewpoint of the child, agreeing to the sexual abuse was an attempt to keep her father from leaving. Therefore, she says to him, "I did it gladly for you, but now I let you go. I will stay with my mother."*

*Feeling her love for her father, she tells him, "Even though you go, you remain in my heart."*

HELLINGER *to Edda* What is your problem?
EDDA I have ovarian cancer.
HELLINGER Anything else?
EDDA And bulimia.
HELLINGER How long have you had bulimia?
EDDA For decades.
HELLINGER And the cancer?
EDDA For three years.
HELLINGER What's the prognosis?
EDDA I think it'll be operable soon. There's a theory that a tumour encapsulates when conflict has been resolved and the thinking changed.

* Course in Munich

HELLINGER  Are you married?

EDDA  Yes.

HELLINGER  Have you got any children?

EDDA  Yes, two sons, 23 and 25 years old.

HELLINGER  Did anything special happen in your family of origin?

EDDA  My father was in the war and I was born in Warsaw at the time when the ghetto was there. My father worked there. He was in the SS.

HELLINGER  And you were born in the ghetto?

EDDA  We lived outside the ghetto, but he worked there. Well, you could scarcely say worked.

HELLINGER  Why was your mother there?

EDDA  My father brought my mother and my sister there in 1942 and established a relatively complete living situation there for his family. I even had a hand-carved cradle. I was born in 1943.

HELLINGER  Was your father tried later?

EDDA  No, but he became seriously ill and was severely depressed. He died three years ago.

HELLINGER  Okay, now we have a connection.

EDDA  I don't know if it has any meaning here, but my father abused my sister and me when we were about 9 and 12 years old.

HELLINGER  We'll set up your family of origin: your father, your mother, and the children.

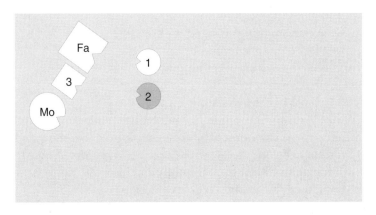

Fa  Father
Mo  Mother
1   First child, a daughter
**2   Second child, a daughter (Edda)**
3   Third child, a son

HELLINGER How's the father feeling?

FATHER Not so well. My wife and son to my right are completely gone and my awareness is centred on my daughters.

MOTHER I feel cut off from the family.

THIRD CHILD It's almost unbearably tense here between my parents. My sisters are looking at me accusingly and it's very unpleasant.

FIRST CHILD I think I've got a very good place here.

SECOND CHILD I feel very close to my father.

HELLINGER *to group* The two daughters are blocking the father's way.

*To father* Leave the room now and close the door behind you.

*To group* Leaving the room means dying or committing suicide.

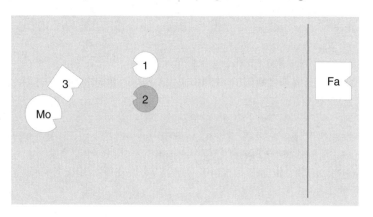

HELLINGER Has anything changed for his wife?

MOTHER I've got more energy.

THIRD CHILD That's a big relief for me.

FIRST CHILD Also better.

SECOND CHILD My heart's beating hard.

HELLINGER *to group* She will follow her father. When something has occurred such as she's described, you can assume that the man has lost his right to belong, because it's the same as murder. A murderer has lost the right to belong to the family and he or she has to leave. If they don't, then the children will leave instead.

*Hellinger asks Edda to take the place of her representative.*

HELLINGER *to Edda* How do you feel?

EDDA *(crying)* Not very good.

*Hellinger puts his arms around her and holds her as she sobs.*

HELLINGER *(after a while) to a group member* Bring the father back in now.
*To father* How was it for you out there?
FATHER Better.
HELLINGER That's the way it is. In this case death is appropriate.
*To Edda* Now turn to your father.
*To father* Take her in your arms.

*The father puts his arms around Edda and she sobs aloud.*

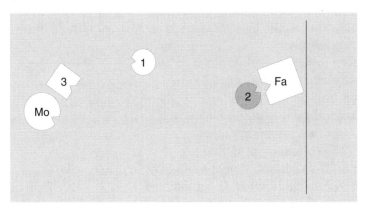

HELLINGER *to Edda* What did you call your father when you were a child?
EDDA Papi.
HELLINGER Say, "Dear Papi."
EDDA Dear Papi.
HELLINGER "Even though you go,"
EDDA Even though you go,
HELLINGER "I'm staying."
EDDA I'm staying.
HELLINGER Repeat it.
EDDA Dear Papi, even though you go, I'm staying.
HELLINGER *(after a while)* Now go and stand next to your mother.

*Hellinger places Edda to the right side of her mother. He moves the other children off to the side.*

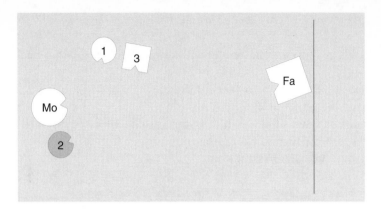

HELLINGER *to Edda* Look at your father and tell him, "I'm staying with my mother."

EDDA I'm staying with my mother.

HELLINGER "This is my place."

EDDA This is my place.

HELLINGER How's that for the mother?

MOTHER Nice. I feel very calm.

HELLINGER And for the father?

FATHER That's how it should be. It's right. I'm also relieved.

HELLINGER *to Edda* What do you say?

EDDA What do I say? I'm doing fine here now.

HELLINGER Okay. That's all.

## SAFETY NEAR HER MOTHER

HELLINGER *to group:* We can see a double dynamic operating here. At one level that is not so apparent, is the dynamic 'I'll follow you.' In the foreground is the dynamic 'Me rather than you, dear Papa.' A child like this is safer next to her mother.

## BACKGROUND OF THE SEXUAL ABUSE

EDDA In the past few years I've often wondered how much my mother knew about what happened with me and my sister. You said recently in a group that the mother is usually indirectly involved in an incest situation.

HELLINGER In this case, I see something else. The two daughters are blocking the way so that the father can't go. They hold him with their love. Both of them loved their father.

*To group* Could you all see that? They didn't feel abused. This dynamic is much too deep to be judged superficially and morally.

EDDA It's true that I loved him very much.

HELLINGER To step free of the abused victim, you have to tell your father: "I did it gladly for you."

*Hellinger calls back the father's representative.*

HELLINGER *to Edda* Tell him, "I did it gladly for you."

EDDA I did it gladly for you.

HELLINGER "But now I let you go."

EDDA But now I let you go.

HELLINGER *(seeing that she is very moved)* Breathe deeply. Say it once more, "Dear Papi, I did it gladly for you. But now I'll let you go."

EDDA But now I'll let you go.

HELLINGER "I'll stay with my mother."

EDDA I'll stay with my mother.

HELLINGER How is it now?

EDDA My heart's beating wildly, I'm sweating, and I've got icy cold feet.

HELLINGER Now tell him, "Even though you go, you remain in my heart."

EDDA Even though you go, you remain in my heart.

HELLINGER How's that?

EDDA My heart's pounding even harder in my throat and my knees are shaking.

HELLINGER That has to work on you for a time. Okay?


## BACKGROUND OF THE BULIMIA

I'd like to say something about the bulimia. Are you still bulimic?

EDDA Yes.

HELLINGER Do you know how you cure that?

EDDA No.

HELLINGER There's a standard approach, but perhaps it's not applicable here. But, in bulimic families it's usually the case that the mother communicates to the children: "Take only from me, what you get from your father is no good."

EDDA But that's true. That's exactly how it was. Yes.

HELLINGER Then the child takes only from the mother, but as revenge, he or she takes too much, and out of love for the father, spits it out again. That evens things up between the parents, because the child loves both parents. What do you say to that?

EDDA It's true. Most of all the sentence, "Don't take from your father."

HELLINGER The standard approach to bulimia is: When the bulimic child is on the verge of an eating binge, she should buy everything and anything she wants, lay it all out on the table and enjoy the sight. Then, she takes a small spoon and imagining that she's sitting on her daddy's lap she begins to eat. Before each mouthful, however, she looks at her daddy and says, "It tastes good with you." This fantasy has cured many of bulimia. Bulimia has another dynamic, particularly when it's coupled with anorexia. Some people suffer from both at the same time.

EDDA That's how it started out.

HELLINGER Anorexia?

EDDA Yes.

HELLINGER Anorexia means, "It's better that I should disappear than you, my dear father."

EDDA That fits exactly.

HELLINGER And when the child eats again, she becomes bulimic. When she eats, she is saying "I'll stay," and when she vomits, she is saying "I'll disappear." She swings between life and death – back

64

and forth, because eating is life and vomiting, death. The healing dynamic would be: When you want to vomit, you say, "Papa, I'm staying."

EDDA  That's what I've said to him, now.

HELLINGER  I think we've brought to light the most important issues in the family.

## RESPECT FOR THE FATHER

HELLINGER *to group*  When there's something as serious as this in a family, the way she described it, then anything else that has happened is of lesser importance. You can forget about anything else, because this serious business draws all the energy. Therefore, I can't work on anything else here.

*To Edda*  Did you see how the father reacted when you said, "I'm staying"?

EDDA  He had a very friendly smile.

HELLINGER  Exactly. Even such fathers have a father's heart.

EDDA  I also loved him.

HELLINGER  Once there was a son of an SS doctor in one of my courses. He wanted to be angry with his father. I said to him, "At the moment of your conception he wasn't in the SS. It had to do with something quite different. Fatherhood is something different, in and of itself."

*To Edda*  You have to respect and take your father as a father. In spite of that, he must go. That's the consequence of his guilt.

Good. That's it.

## VICTIMS AND PERPETRATORS

QUESTION  You said that if someone within the family system has killed someone, the murderer loses the right to belong. But you also said that it's different in the case of abuse, that the abuser doesn't lose the right to belong. What's the case with family violence, for example, when a man throws his wife through a window?

HELLINGER  Then he's lost his right to belong. Anything that is in the direction of an attempt to kill, or a threat of murder has the same effect.

QUESTION  And what does it mean that he must go? You said that when you send someone out of the room, it means suicide or going.

HELLINGER It means that no one may stand in his way when he goes. His wife can't kill herself in his place, nor can the children commit suicide in his place, nor can anyone become ill or have an accident in his place. That's the main message. One has to leave the consequences of the act with the person who committed the act. A person who has done such a thing must carry the consequences and the guilt, and can never be freed from them.

The perpetrator must carry the guilt. For example, if the father, in this case, had said, 'I'm guilty and I face my guilt,' and if he had then left his family to spare them the burden of his guilt, and if he had done something worthy, that would have been a way of coming to terms with the crime and a form of redress. The guilt is not erased, but he could have regained some of his dignity. It's also easier for the victims to be reconciled with the perpetrator and the situation if they see that some good has been done to honour them. That would have been the solution here.

QUESTION It disturbs me that you also call this blind devotion love, even though it has such terrible effects.

HELLINGER Yes, it's love. The other love, that resolves, draws strength from this blind love. The love remains the same, only the awareness changes. Then there's an inner departure from the magical thinking that one can take over the consequences of guilt for someone else. Taking over the consequences of someone else's guilt prevents a balancing out at a higher level. A resolution is only possible when the magical thinking is relinquished and the consequences remain with the guilty.

You could see in this case that the father is reconciled with his daughter if she stays. In blind love, a person is willing to die for someone else out of love, without seeing that the other person also loves. If this love of the other can be seen and acknowledged, the wish to die as a substitute subsides.

That's why, in this work, when someone is drawn to follow another into death, or to die in place of another, the most important method is to allow the person to see and be seen by the other and to repeat the sentence, "Better I should die than you." If the person can truly look the other in the eye while saying this sentence, he or she will realize that it's impossible because love also comes from the other. This removes the blindness from the love, but the love remains.

The perpetrator is relieved if no loved one dies in his or her place, and the child is relieved because he or she can love but need not die.

QUESTION You said that the victims can be reconciled, in this case, the Ghetto victims. Is it also the case that magical thinking leads to the belief that revenge will appease the victims?

HELLINGER No. They can be reconciled in so far as no one who is innocent suffers or dies because of the crime that was perpetrated against them.

The perpetrator cannot be reconciled with the victims, for example, by asking for forgiveness, even if he or she follows the path of doing something worthy as atonement. This is not because the dead demand revenge. They are on a different level altogether. Revenge won't appease the dead, but rather honour and grief. I'm talking now about the partners and descendants of a perpetrator.

It's a different situation with the partners and descendants of the victims. For example, if a father experiences the death of his wife and one of his children through a bicycle accident, due to the recklessness of a speeding Porsche driver, then he, as a survivor, is as much a victim as his wife and child. If the father, however, concentrates on the perpetrator with outrage and a desire for revenge, he is unable to grieve. The wrath, accusations, and demands for retribution block the grief. The result is that the survivor cannot say farewell to the dead and none of them come to a place of peace. The attention is drawn to the perpetrator and away from the dead. The grief and love of the dead ones also cannot be recognized, because the father is not looking at them, nor they at him. They are unable to say farewell to him, and are not free to be dead, and he is not free to live whatever life is left to him to live. The perpetrator is also unable to grieve and through grief to come to a reconciliation with the dead.

It's even worse if someone who is not directly affected takes on the outrage as if they were the victim, instead of looking at the dead with honour and grief. Or when those who belong to the same race or nationality are joined to the perpetrators and accused – then they are also unable to grieve.

For example, when a German goes into the memorial for the victims of the Holocaust in Jerusalem and sees what was done to these people; normally, it is shattering and he or she weeps. It is so horrible that there is no alternative but to weep for the victims. If, however, someone says to him or her, "You're a German," then grieving is no longer possible, even if the person is personally innocent.

The same is true of Hiroshima. When someone goes into the memorial for the victims of the atomic bomb attack, he or she has to weep. People stand there in front of the pictures and the tears flow. If someone then says, "You're an American," the grieving stops.

The dead are reconciled through our pain when we weep in front of them. That is reconciling. If we can do something of value in memory of the dead, then the strength from the dead enters into the good that we do. That has a reconciling effect at a deeper level. However, if someone gets busily involved, calling for action, without really having the dead in their thoughts and before their eyes, then there's very little reconciling energy.

QUESTION  Is the perpetrator exonerated in this way?

HELLINGER  No, that's not possible. A perpetrator cannot be exonerated, even by doing good things. The guilt remains. With such serious crimes the guilt remains forever, and any attempt to take it away is a devaluation of both the perpetrator and the victims.

QUESTION  But you've said that the father of this family has to leave the family so that the victims can be reconciled.

HELLINGER  He has to leave because of his family, not because of the victims. He can rescue his children so they don't have to follow him or try to hold him back when he leaves. That's the primary issue here. Leaving the family, however, often means that he then goes to join the dead – that he dies himself and lies next to them. If he faces his guilt in this way and acts accordingly, then he honours the victims as well.

QUESTION  It concerns me that you said that this father has lost his right to live. I could imagine a man who was in the SS who performed his duty with great pangs of conscience and survived because he was allowed to survive. But you said that this father has lost his right to belong.

HELLINGER  The way the woman described it, her father had a high ranking. He was high enough up in rank to bring his wife and children with him. Such a person carries a heavy personal responsibility. Therefore, I imagine that one cannot absolve him. I don't know anything more about it.

### LETTER FROM A PARTICIPANT IN A LATER SEMINAR

Since the last course, I've got a completely new feeling towards my grandfather, who was imprisoned for his Nazi activities. His representative was sent out of the room during a family constellation.

It is so good to see him lying next to the victims. I am more capable of regard for him and can leave him in peace. The feeling is very peaceful, and it can now truly be laid to rest. As the representative for my grandfather walked out of the door, I still had a tinge of guilt, but this new image has a different effect. That's also because I've been a representative in other constellations.

It was very good for me to bow down before the victims and the perpetrators together.

# Ruth*
## Both parents were in a concentration camp, her grandparents and two uncles died in the camp

### SUMMARY

The entanglements: *Ruth has an eating disorder and is starving herself. Both her parents were in a concentration camp but survived. Her grandparents and two uncles were killed in the camp. Her eldest sister died at the age of one month, and Ruth is primarily identified with her.*

The resolution: *The dead grandparents are brought into view. Both parents lean back against their own parents, experience the pain and feel relieved. They can then also turn to their own children and grandchildren. The child who died so young feels excluded. She finds security in the family only when her parents stand together and she sits in front of them, leaning back against them. Ruth says to her dead sister, "Dear Helenka, I have missed you."*

*The dead sister stands next to Ruth. The two sisters hold each other and Ruth sobs loudly. She looks at her sister and says, "You have a place in my heart. In me, you'll still live a while, and then I'll come too."*

*The mother's two dead brothers are brought into the picture. Ruth approaches each of the dead, looks into their eyes, and bows down to them. Finally, she returns to her place with her siblings.*

HELLINGER *to Ruth*  How are you doing?
RUTH  I'm a little anxious.
HELLINGER  Could you say briefly what the difficulty is?
RUTH  I have an eating disorder. Whenever I eat and am aware of food in my stomach, and when I am supposed to go to work, I with-

* Course in Munich

draw to the toilet and really would prefer just to stay there. It's not always that extreme, but the wish is there. I often have diarrhoea, and I don't know if that's moving in the direction of anorexia. I suspect that I'm a latent anorexic. Sometimes I feel like I would like to starve to death. I've experienced a lot of violence in my family and I've got a very negative symbiosis with my mother. Her messages accompany my every step. That's why nothing succeeds in my life. I was able to get an education, but with anything that belongs to life, family, or work, it's impossible for me to succeed.

HELLINGER  What happened in your family of origin?

RUTH  My parents were in a concentration camp. I was raised as a victim and I punish myself all the time. I would like to find out why I always punish myself. I always have stomachache.

HELLINGER  Did someone die?

RUTH  Yes. My mother's parents and two of her brothers died in the concentration camp. On my father's side, his parents died and his sister survived hidden in Vienna. My first sister was born in 1964 and died after a month.

HELLINGER  Of what?

RUTH  I don't know. But for the past year, I've been angry with her for leaving me alone. That's very new.

HELLINGER  Are your parents separated?

RUTH  No, they stuck it out together. My father died ten years ago and my mother is still alive.

HELLINGER  That's a heavy fate. I'll do my best. Okay?

RUTH  Yes, yes.

HELLINGER  Choose representatives for your parents, yourself, and your siblings and place them in relation to one another.

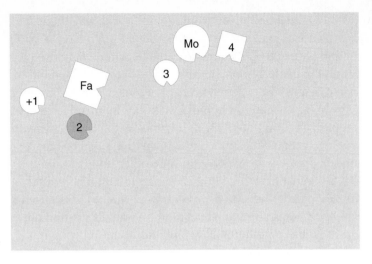

Fa   Father
Mo   Mother
1      First child, a daughter (died at the age of one month)
**2      Second child, a daughter (Ruth)**
3      Third child, a daughter
4      Fourth child, a son

HELLINGER How is the father doing?
FATHER I've got a pain in my right shoulder and I feel strange in this place.
HELLINGER How's the mother?
MOTHER I don't feel like I'm in my place. I have no relationship – the strongest is to my second daughter.
HELLINGER How is the dead sister?
FIRST CHILD I don't belong here.
HELLINGER *to Ruth's representative* How are you?
RUTH'S REPRESENTATIVE Odd. My father seems more like my brother. Behind me there's security. There's absolutely nothing with my mother or siblings.
HELLINGER How is the younger sister?
THIRD CHILD I feel penned in here. I don't want to stand so close to my mother, I'd rather go over to my father.
FOURTH CHILD I feel neutral, but restless. I'd like to go somewhere over to the left.

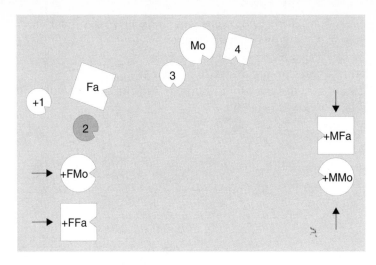

FFa  Father's father (died in concentration camp)
FMo  Father's mother (died in concentration camp)
MFa  Mother's father (died in concentration camp)
MMo  Mother's mother (died in concentration camp)

*Hellinger has added representatives for the grandparents who died in the concentration camp.*

HELLINGER  What has changed for the father?
FATHER  I'm cold. As my parents came in, I went rigid.

*Hellinger places him with his back to his parents and has him lean back against them.*

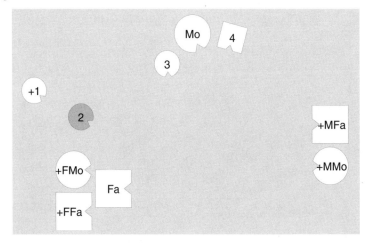

HELLINGER *to father who is crying* Now the pain comes. Let it in.
*After a while* Stay there a while longer.
*To mother* What has changed for you?
MOTHER I feel strongly drawn to my parents.
HELLINGER Do the same thing. Stand with your back to your parents and lean back against them.

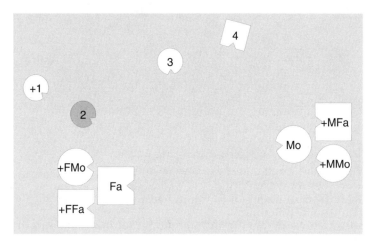

HELLINGER *after a while to Ruth's representative* How are you now?
RUTH'S REPRESENTATIVE Lighter. Before I had a strange pull toward my father and that's gone now – it's moved to the right to my grandparents. I could feel his pain. Suddenly I wasn't sure if my sister was still behind me and I had to turn around and look.

*Hellinger places the children next to one another.*

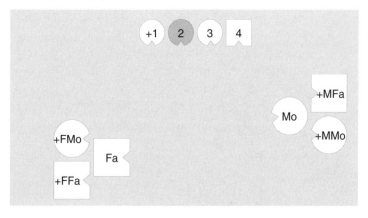

74

HELLINGER *to father*  How are you doing now?

FATHER  It's very warm behind me. Good. Very good.

HELLINGER *to mother*  How are things with you?

MOTHER  Also better at my back. And now I feel a connection with my husband.

HELLINGER *to dead child*  How are you doing now?

FIRST CHILD  Since my mother has moved there, I've felt very anxious and my heart has started beating very hard. Since I've been standing with my brother and sisters, it's a bit better.

RUTH'S REPRESENTATIVE  It's good, but sad.

THIRD CHILD  I feel better here. Since my mother moved away, I've felt much better. My entire left side was stiff while my mother was there.

FOURTH CHILD  It was just the same for me. I only noticed when my mother moved away that I had been carrying her the whole time. Now I can move freely again.

HELLINGER  How are the grandparents feeling?

FATHER'S FATHER  It's good like this. It's good that he's there.

FATHER'S MOTHER  Before my son came, it was very comfortable on my right, very warm. I would have liked to have moved over further towards my husband. When my son came over, I could hardly breathe, and it was only as he began to cry that I felt better. When the second daughter moved away, it got very cold here on my left. On the right side it's very warm and comfortable, but over here it's completely cold.

HELLINGER *to Ruth*  The dead don't do well if there is no pain at their leaving. Your father wasn't able to express his pain over the deaths of his parents because it was too great. But you could see how it affects your grandmother when he can't express his pain. Pain is actually an expression of great love.

HELLINGER  How are the other grandparents doing?

MOTHER'S FATHER  At first my pulse was racing, but now I'm looking so happily at my grandchildren.

MOTHER'S MOTHER  It's the same for me. My knees still hurt and I feel like I want to give my children and grandchildren something.

*Hellinger puts the parents together. The child who died young is seated with her back to her parents, leaning against them. The other children stand together opposite the parents and dead sister.*

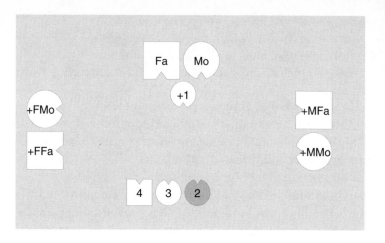

HELLINGER *to the parents* Lay your hand gently on the child's head. *To the dead child* How is it there for you?

FIRST CHILD Very secure.

HELLINGER *to Ruth's representative* How are you?

RUTH'S REPRESENTATIVE I felt sad and now that's gone.

HELLINGER How's the father doing now?

FATHER I have a very strong connection with this girl.

MOTHER I feel rather sad towards this dead child. Towards my husband, fine. And it's also fine with my other children now that I can see them.

*Hellinger places the grandparents nearer to their children.*

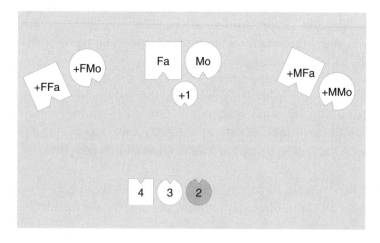

RUTH'S REPRESENTATIVE  I'd like to take my dead sister in my arms.

HELLINGER *to Ruth*  The primary identification is with your dead sister. There you can see the power of those who died young. It overshadows even this other heavy fate. Take your place in the constellation.

RUTH *as she stands in her place*  In the last year, I've suddenly started having conversations with her. I asked her why she abandoned me. I'm so unprotected. She abandoned me.

HELLINGER  She died. That's it.

RUTH  She died and I had to pay.

HELLINGER  Look at her. What's her name?

RUTH  Helenka, Helena.

HELLINGER  You can speak to her in your mother tongue. Say, "My dear Helenka."

RUTH  I'll speak to her in German. My dear Helenka.

HELLINGER  Look at her with love.

RUTH  I am so angry with her. *(She cries.)*

HELLINGER  Look at her with love. Anger is the flip side of love. See how touched she is. See how she is looking at you with love. Tell her, "I've missed you."

RUTH  I've missed you.

*Ruth is very moved. After a while Hellinger moves the dead sister to Ruth. The sisters take each other in their arms and Ruth sobs loudly.*

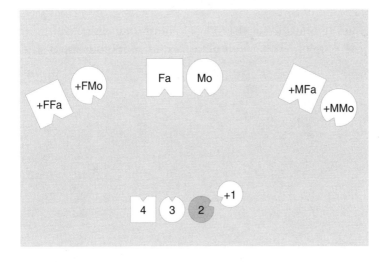

HELLINGER *(after a while) to Ruth* Breathe deeply; inhale and exhale deeply. Let the pain flow deeply. Let the tears flow.

RUTH *(after a while)* I'm dizzy, but my sister is holding me.

HELLINGER Now breathe without any sound. Very simply, in and out. Now it can flow.

*After a while* Look at your sister. Look at her. Take both her hands, look at her and tell her, "You have a place in my heart."

RUTH You have a place in my heart.

HELLINGER *(as she weeps)* Look at her, clearly and without emotion. Look at her and say, "You have a place in my heart."

RUTH You have a place in my heart.

HELLINGER "In me you'll still live a little while."

RUTH In me you'll still live a little while.

HELLINGER "Then I'll come too."

RUTH Then I'll come too.

HELLINGER "You have a place in my heart."

RUTH You have a place in my heart.

HELLINGER "In me you'll still live a little while."

RUTH In me you'll still live a little while.

HELLINGER "Together with me."

RUTH Together with me.

HELLINGER "Then I'll come too."

RUTH Then I'll come too. Where? She's dead. In Heaven, or what?

HELLINGER I'll leave it like that. Whatever it is. But it has a comforting effect.

*To group* It's clear to see that it has a comforting effect.

*To dead sister* Now take your place next to your brother and sisters.

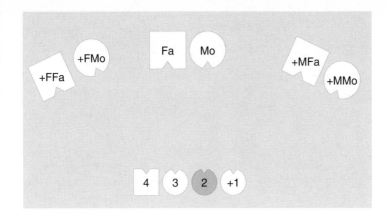

HELLINGER *to dead sister* How are you feeling?
FIRST CHILD Good.
HELLINGER How are the others?
THIRD CHILD Good.
FOURTH CHILD There's no contact with my elder sister there *(Ruth)*. I would make contact with her, but I have the feeling that she doesn't want that.
HELLINGER Stand next to your father. How is it for you there?
FOURTH CHILD I can see her.
HELLINGER *to Ruth* I think your brother has to stay next to his father for a while. He needs his father for a time. How is your brother doing, really?
RUTH Hard to say.

*Hellinger puts the brother back with his sisters and leads Ruth in front of him.*

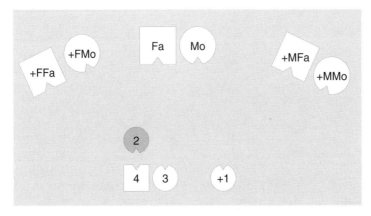

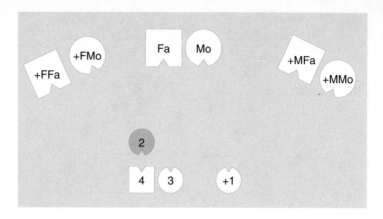

HELLINGER *to Ruth* Look at him and tell him, "I'm your big sister."
RUTH I'm your big sister.
HELLINGER "And you're my little brother."
RUTH And you're my little brother.
HELLINGER *to brother* How's that for you?
Fourth Child Finally.
RUTH I feel ill. I feel nauseous.
HELLINGER Then go a little closer to him. Look him in the eye.

*As she is unable to do this, Hellinger brings representatives into the constellation for the mother's two brothers who both died in the concentration camp.*

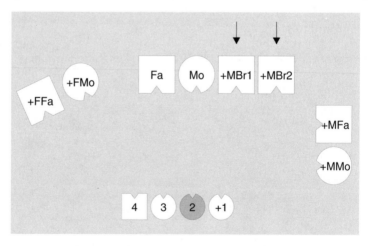

MBr1    Mother's first brother (died in concentration camp)
MBr2    Mother's second brother (died in concentration camp)

HELLINGER *to mother* How is it for you when they're here?

Mother I'm closer to my dead parents, and the relationship to my children is very alive. I feel warmth towards my husband.

HELLINGER *to father* What has changed for you since they've come in?

Father It's a bit lighter, only, I'm aware that my daughter has become very restless.

HELLINGER *to Ruth* I suspect that your relationship to your brother mirrors the relationship of your mother to her brothers. If they're in sight, can you look at your brother?

RUTH No, I can't. Not easily.

HELLINGER *to group* I wonder where these feelings are coming from? They have been taken over from somewhere else. Now we have to look for the source.

*Hellinger places Ruth between her mother and the mother's dead brothers.*

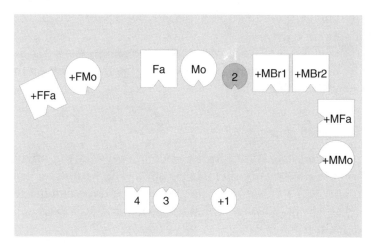

HELLINGER *to Ruth* How's that?

RUTH I feel like I want to throw up. It's not bad and I feel stable, but I'm just saying I feel like I want to throw up.

HELLINGER I'll do an exercise with you. Go to each of the dead persons in turn and, looking at them, bow down before them with love.

*Ruth goes to the representatives of the dead and, looking each in the eye, bows before them. She bows to her dead sister as well and then returns to her place with her siblings.*

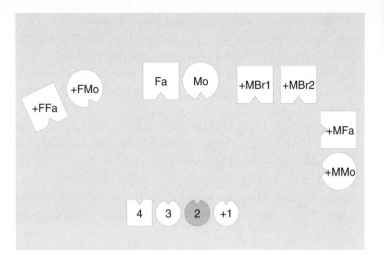

HELLINGER  How are you now?

RUTH  My nausea is a bit better. I'm very sad about my sister, I feel that very strongly.

HELLINGER  Somewhere, there's something still missing. We don't know what it is, but perhaps it'll come up later. We'll leave it there for now. Okay, that's all.

### HONOURING THE DEAD

HELLINGER *to group*  When there's such a heavy fate, the survivors often have a feeling of guilt for being alive. What's called for then is solidarity with the dead. First, there needs to be respect for the dead, which is why the bowing down is so important. And, it's also important that they are looked at.

Both parents are drawn to their own parents, which you could see plainly in the constellation. They were very clearly separated at the beginning, but when their parents were in view, they could come together.

*To Ruth*  Then, on top of that came the fate of your sister. There are other things operating in the family, but we don't need to look at them now. There's a good energy which is having effects now. You have to hold all of them in your heart: your grandparents, your dead uncles, and your dead sister. And then, that sentence I told you is very important, "Then I'll die too." That removes the feeling of su-

82

periority over the dead. "I'll live a bit longer" and "You'll live a little while longer in me." Life is only a short time compared to death. Through this humility, you can feel at one with the dead and so can stay alive. It takes the arrogance out of life. Do you understand that now?

RUTH  Yes.

HELLINGER  What do you owe the dead?

RUTH  That I stay alive.

HELLINGER  Exactly. That's what you owe. That's honouring the dead. They look kindly on you when you're alive and healthy.

RUTH  That's fine. I understand.


## FOLLOW-UP COMMENTARY

RUTH *on the following day to the group*  This is the first time that I've spoken in front of so many people. Yesterday you all experienced how sad I was about my sister. I want to say briefly what's happened for me. I feel very relieved. When I was a child, they always said, "You're the eldest," and I always had the feeling I carried the burden of my parents' terrible marriage as the eldest and the most sensible. Now I feel very relieved. I know now what that was. The position of eldest belonged to my sister. As of today, I'm the second eldest and that fits for me. I can take care of my own life without that pressure. For that, I want to say thank you. *(Applause in the group)*


## THE LIVING AND THE DEAD

QUESTION  Where do you believe the dead are?

HELLINGER  When someone dies, they are not gone. They have an effect in the system as long as there's a memory of them still alive. After that they're really dead. You can see though, that when the dead are acknowledged, they can move bit by bit into the background, and what is past can be past.

When the dead from the concentration camp and Ruth's dead sister could be seen and bowed down to, then the dead could retreat into the background, as though to make room for the living.

QUESTION  What does that mean, that the dead can be seen?

HELLINGER  First, literally, that the representatives of the dead are put into the constellation so that the others can look at them. It also means, however, allowing an internal image of the dead person to appear and looking into the eyes of the dead.

Many people are reluctant to look at the dead because it's so painful. But if you are able to really look at the dead, it has a comforting, strengthening effect.

RUTH You said that the dead have an effect as long as we remember them. But then you said that when the dead are acknowledged they go away. How do you explain that?

HELLINGER When the dead are acknowledged, they move into the background, as the sun shines from afar. They are no longer a burden. They stand at a distance, but are present in a benevolent way. In this sunshine, you can open up.

RUTH And what about the grief work?

HELLINGER You've seen here what grief work is, for example, with the representatives for your father and your mother, and you've experienced it yourself. But now you can't keep working on it. You can't go back into the constellation.

The secret of this way is that you move forward, leaving everything behind you. Sometimes you hold on because something isn't finished, but now you've finished something and you can move on.

## FAMILY AND ILLNESS

QUESTION This is a course about systemic psychosomatic illness, but you didn't address the issue of illness at all in the last constellation.

HELLINGER Many people understand systemic psychosomatic illness as if the attention should be focused primarily on the illness. What you've noticed is that I don't pay so much attention to the illness nor to whether or not someone is cured, I work with the system. I look to see if there are things having an effect that may cause illness. These are the things I want to bring into the open. More precisely, I look to see if there are people in the system who may cause illness because they are excluded or not respected. If so, I bring them back in, and when they are included and respected, they have a healing effect.

What actually happens with an illness is not as important to me, because my work is in the system. That has implications for the illness, but I don't follow them. That has to do with this particular way of working and the underlying basis. I can only work in this way if I move into the system and the energy field of the system. As soon as a client approaches me, gives me the basic information, and sets up a constellation, I am suddenly in an energy field. I then use myself, my perception, and my knowledge to bring a healing or reconciling movement in the system. Then I move back out of the field and leave it to its own dynamic. If I were to remain in the system, I would disturb the movement of the system. For example, if I were to inquire later about what has happened, I would move into the field again, not being directed by the field, but on my own initiative, wanting to check on the success, as if the result was due to me. Therefore, I don't do that. I trust the forces which direct me and the client, and I obey them.

There's something else to be considered here. The therapist breaks off at the strongest point. That's when the soul has the greatest energy, and if the therapist pulls back, this strength remains.

............

# Horst*
## His grandfather held a leading SS position in the Dachau concentration camp

### COMMENT

As this constellation was rather long and complicated, only the summary is included here.

### SUMMARY

The entanglements: *Horst is diabetic. His mother is with him at the seminar. His maternal grandfather held an important SS position in the Dachau concentration camp. As an officer's wife, his maternal grandmother led a life of leisure, which is implied in a photo of her relaxing at the swimming pool, with the fence of the concentration camp in the background. Horst's mother was born after the war. His mother's brother starved at the age of one month in a prison camp due to a milk shortage. Horst is primarily identified with his mother's dead brother. It remains unclear to what extent Horst and his mother are influenced by the fate of her parents.*

The resolution: *The mother's parents were sent out of the room, where they felt better. The mother is drawn to follow her parent; Horst to his mother's dead brother. His mother says to her dead brother, "Be friendly to me if I remain. And be friendly if my son remains."*

### WHEN HAS SOMEONE LOST THEIR RIGHT TO BELONG?

QUESTION  When have parents lost their right to belong?
HELLINGER  When have they lost their rights? I'll put it this way: Whenever the person is involved in a serious crime. Serious crimes include

---

\* Course in Munich

86

murder, attempted murder, or the threat of murder. A threat would have to be seriously intended.

QUESTION  What about murder in a war, like fathers who were soldiers in a war. You can assume that some of their shots hit the mark and killed someone.

HELLINGER  It depends. Fighting in a war, in and of itself, doesn't have this effect, but if the action were, for example, against prisoners, then it would have this effect.


## ABORTION

QUESTION  Is abortion also murder?

HELLINGER  Abortion doesn't have the same effect in the system as murder, but parents who have had an abortion often punish themselves severely. They pay for it. With an abortion, the child gives everything and the parents take everything. The child gives its life and the parents take their freedom. Then the parents inwardly balance things out, often in direct opposition to the stated reason for the abortion. The soul doesn't listen to reasons. The most common way of evening things is that the relationship is over. As a rule, after an abortion, a relationship is finished. That's the first step. The second is that they often can't find or keep new relationships. Particularly the woman often doesn't trust herself to take a man. Or, they restrict themselves in some other way.

QUESTION  What about when a woman wants to have an abortion but doesn't do it?

HELLINGER  Intentions don't count, only the results. The main question here is what the parents can do to set things right.

The first thing is that the child has to be seen as a child. That is, the parents look at this child as their child. The mother can, for example, say to the child, "My dear child, you are my child and I am your mother. You've made room for me so that things will be better for me. I accept that from you as a gift." That goes very deep. And when the pain comes up, over the death of this child, it reconciles. That deep, deep pain reconciles.

Then the mother and the father take the child into their hearts and give it a peaceful place to rest. In memory of the child and with the strength of their guilt, they can do something worthy.

When something like this has come up, life is never again as it was before, it has a new seriousness and depth. An ardent relationship like a first love, for example, is no longer possible. When the parents who have aborted a child feel this pain, they can turn to one another again, but it is no longer the same relationship as before. The relationship has a different depth and a different seriousness.

After an abortion, though, it's important that the guilt be allowed to end. Hanging on to guilt is arrogant. So, after a while there must be peace for everyone.

# Joscha*
## His grandfather was in the SS

## SUMMARY

The entanglements: *Joscha is six years old and has an asthmatic allergy, and is particularly sensitive to horses. He is accompanied by his parents. His paternal grandfather was in the SS Horse Division. His father's sister was killed in a car accident.*

The resolution: *The father's father was sent out of the room. The father feels relieved, as does his sister and his ill son. Because the family system of the father is burdened by the grandfather, the children are placed within their mother's sphere. In his position outside, the grandfather feels relieved, but experiences some chest symptoms.*

HELLINGER *to the parents* What is this about?
WIFE Joscha is six years old and has allergic asthma. Since he was two, he's had croup-like attacks. He reacts very strongly to horses and his eyes swell shut. We haven't been able to find out what brings on these bronchial attacks and we're worried.
HELLINGER What does the father have to say?
HUSBAND In principle, the same.
HELLINGER How many children have you got?
HUSBAND Four.
HELLINGER And which one is he?
HUSBAND The eldest.
HELLINGER *to wife* Set up the present family system: you, your wife, and the four children.

* Course in Munich

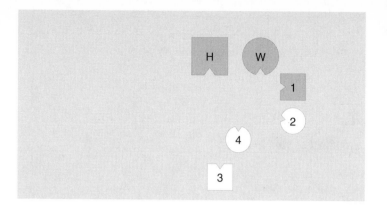

HELLINGER *to wife* Did anything happen at the birth of your first child?

WIFE No, it was a quick birth. He was almost born in the car, but there were no complications.

HELLINGER How is the husband feeling?

HUSBAND'S REPRESENTATIVE My youngest daughter is blocking my way. To the right, here in front, I have the feeling that something is calling me from a distance. That is, there's something in the distance that is calling.

HELLINGER How's the wife doing?

WIFE'S REPRESENTATIVE I'm very isolated from him and am focused on my youngest daughter. I'm not aware of the other children.

JOSCHA'S REPRESENTATIVE I feel a tightness in my chest. Everything is very closed in. On my right it's very cold, on my left it's rather warm.

HELLINGER *to group* So, he has the symptoms of the actual child. How's the second child feeling?

SECOND CHILD I feel very cheerful. I don't feel very closely connected. I'm just watching it all and I'm aware of it all.

HELLINGER *to third child* How are you?

THIRD CHILD Since the first touch, even before the constellation, I haven't been able to hear anything on the left side. I can't look at anyone and I feel very much on the outside. I've got cold hands.

FOURTH CHILD I just want to leave, out to the right. I've got ice-cold fingers and I felt a whole lot better before next to my mother. Although I feel in the middle of things here, I haven't got a relationship with anyone.

HELLINGER *to husband* What happened in your family of origin? Did anything drastic happen?

HUSBAND Many things. I lost my home when I was a child, and grew up in an emotionally cool environment.

HELLINGER I don't need that kind of thing. I need facts and events. Did anyone die at an early age?

HUSBAND My eldest sister, when I was 13. My father, when I was 15. The elder brother closest to me, when I was 22.

HELLINGER What did your sister die of?

HUSBAND In a car accident, along with my cousin. They were both killed in the accident.

HELLINGER How old was she?

HUSBAND 21.

HELLINGER We'll add a representative for the elder sister.

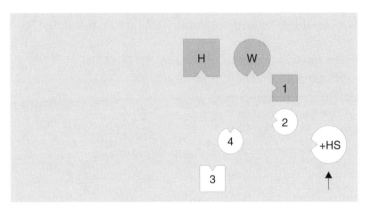

HS  Husband's sister (died at 21 in car accident)

HELLINGER What has changed?

JOSCHA'S REPRESENTATIVE I suddenly have a new orientation – towards her – and I'm also a bit warmer.

HELLINGER *to wife's representative* Has anything changed for you?

WIFE'S REPRESENTATIVE Not much. It's pretty much the same.

HELLINGER *to husband's representative* Has anything changed for you?

HUSBAND'S REPRESENTATIVE At the most, my interest. There's no pull that way.

HELLINGER *to husband's dead sister* How are you feeling?

HUSBAND'S SISTER I'm excited.

HELLINGER *to husband* What else happened in your family? Your father died early. Of what?

HUSBAND My father died of a stroke and pneumonia.

HELLINGER How old was he?

HUSBAND 66.

HELLINGER Was your father married before?

HUSBAND No, no, my father only married once, and relatively late.

HELLINGER *to wife* What do you have to say about that?

WIFE I keep thinking about him, because I think there was something with his father, that he was a storm trooper or something like that. That's all very vague for me, I don't know what role his father played.

HELLINGER *to husband* What was that?

HUSBAND My father was assigned to a division of the Waffen SS, and otherwise was a civil servant. He was with the cavalry SS, a subdivision of the Waffen SS.

HELLINGER If he was with the cavalry SS, then he was in the SS.

*Hellinger moves the husband's dead sister next to her brother. He moves the youngest daughter next to her elder brother.*

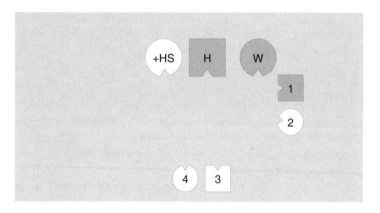

HELLINGER What has changed?

HUSBAND'S REPRESENTATIVE That's good – to be able to see the row of children. That brings strength.

WIFE'S REPRESENTATIVE That's a whole different thing because I can see the children now. But I still can't see the eldest one well enough.

HELLINGER *to eldest child* Has anything changed for you?

JOSCHA'S REPRESENTATIVE I'm still having difficulty breathing.

*Hellinger adds a representative for the husband's father.*

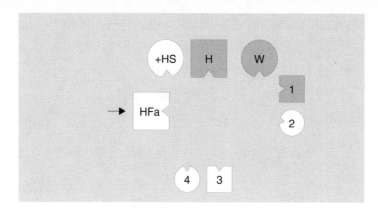

HFa   Husband's father (was in the SS)

HELLINGER *to eldest child* What's happened?
JOSCHA'S REPRESENTATIVE I'm very drawn to him. I feel pushed forwards towards him.
HELLINGER Go over there to him.

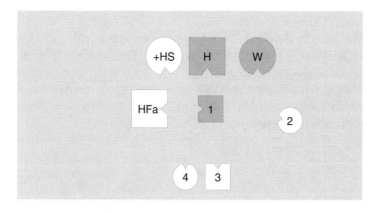

HELLINGER How are things for the husband?
HUSBAND'S REPRESENTATIVE I notice I can't look at him. There's something there that makes me very anxious. I can't look at my father.
HUSBAND'S SISTER It's the same for me. I'm also afraid of him.
HUSBAND'S FATHER I'm warm and otherwise fine.
HELLINGER *to husband* When the others carry it, he can feel fine.

*To group* You have to have loving children and grandchildren to step into the breach, then you can feel fine.

*Hellinger places the husband's father further out and his deceased daughter next to him. He moves the eldest child further away.)*

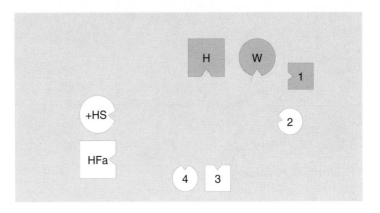

HELLINGER *to husband's father* How is it for you there?

HUSBAND'S FATHER *(clutching his hand to his chest)* There's something in my chest.

HELLINGER What?

HUSBAND'S FATHER Hollow.

HELLINGER *to husband's deceased sister* How about you?

HUSBAND'S SISTER It's better than next to my brother, but I'd like to be a bit further away from him.

HELLINGER *to husband's representative* How are you doing?

HUSBAND'S REPRESENTATIVE I want to hold on to my wife so I won't have to go over there too.

*Hellinger moves him next to his dead sister.*

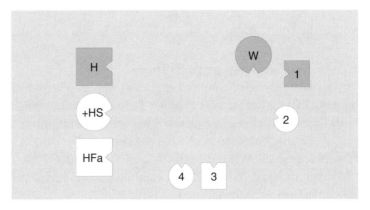

HELLINGER *to eldest child* How is it for you with your father gone?
JOSCHA'S REPRESENTATIVE It's difficult to say. When my grandfather said that he felt something in his chest, I broke out in a sweat. That's still there. It's a little bit easier with my father gone.
HELLINGER That's why your safe place is with your mother. The children have to be in the mother's sphere of influence.

*Hellinger moves the mother somewhat off to the side and the children into a row opposite her.*

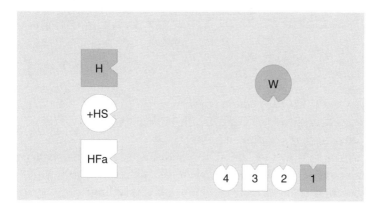

WIFE'S REPRESENTATIVE I was very relieved when my son came back to me. Since then I've felt very excited. Now there's some order. My eldest son is now in view.
JOSCHA'S REPRESENTATIVE I'm not standing quite solidly, but it's better.
HELLINGER *to husband's father* Leave the room. *As he leaves, his deceased daughter breathes out in relief.*
HELLINGER *to group* Aha. Did you see that?

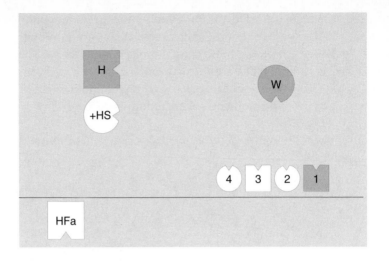

HELLINGER  What has changed?

JOSCHA'S REPRESENTATIVE  I can breathe a little easier.

SECOND CHILD  It's got much lighter.

THIRD CHILD  Now I feel good, too, standing so close in between my brother and sisters and being able to see my mother. Very good.

HELLINGER *to youngest daughter*  How are you feeling?

FOURTH CHILD  Now that I can see my mother I feel really good. I've got a relationship with her now. I still have no relationship with my father.

WIFE'S REPRESENTATIVE  Yes, I feel fine with my four children.

HELLINGER *to husband*  Your family system is burdened, and that has an effect on the child. The question is how to rescue him. I'm trying my best, as you can see.

*To husband's representative*  What's going on now with the husband?

HUSBAND'S REPRESENTATIVE  I'm starting to feel alive. Before, I felt like I was standing on a scaffold. Now that my father is out of here, *(breathes out loudly)* I can live.

HELLINGER *to group*  Who should have the feeling of standing on a scaffold?

GROUP MEMBER  His father.

HELLINGER  Exactly.


*Hellinger moves the husband next to his wife with the children more in the wife's sphere.*

96

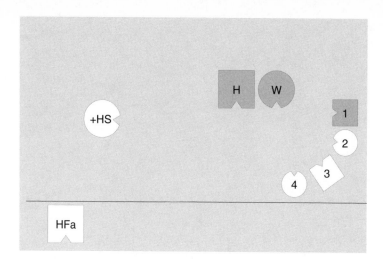

HELLINGER *to the children* You have to get out of your father's sphere.

FOURTH CHILD As he walked past me, I felt a cold wave wash over me. Now that I'm more on my mother's side, I feel better.

HELLINGER That's the sphere of influence. It changes that.

THIRD CHILD I feel just as good as before.

SECOND CHILD Me too. I notice, though, that I'm worried about my father.

JOSCHA'S REPRESENTATIVE I was really glad that Papa came back. *(laughs)*

HELLINGER *to husband's representative* How do you feel?

HUSBAND'S REPRESENTATIVE Just fine.

*Hellinger moves the husband's dead sister near to him.*

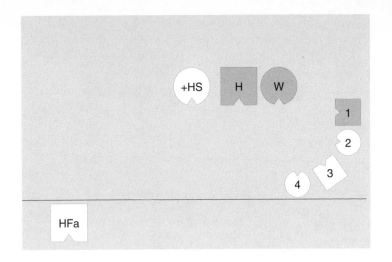

HELLINGER *to husband's dead sister* How is that for you there?
HUSBAND'S SISTER It's good. I was sad when he left.
HELLINGER Has anything changed for anyone else since she moved here?
JOSCHA'S REPRESENTATIVE My heart's pounding a bit harder.

*Hellinger moves him closer to his mother.*

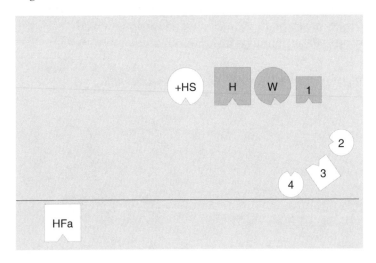

HELLINGER How's that?
JOSCHA'S REPRESENTATIVE Better.

WIFE'S REPRESENTATIVE I wanted to turn to my son. My husband seems a bit of a burden since he's come. I was happy that he came, but he weighs me down a bit.

HELLINGER I noticed you turning towards your son.

*To wife* Did anything unusual happen in your family of origin?

WIFE My mother died of cancer when I was 13. That was the most important thing.

*Hellinger adds a representative for the wife's mother and places her next to the wife's representative.*

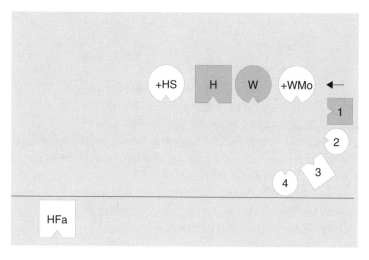

Wmo      Wife's mother (died when her daughter was 13)

HELLINGER *to wife's representative* How is it now?

WIFE'S REPRESENTATIVE Lighter. My whole body is lighter  my shoulders, my neck, everything is lighter. But she doesn't have to be quite so close.

HELLINGER *to wife's mother* How do you feel?

WIFE'S MOTHER It's nice.

*Hellinger moves the mother so that she's standing half behind her daughter.*

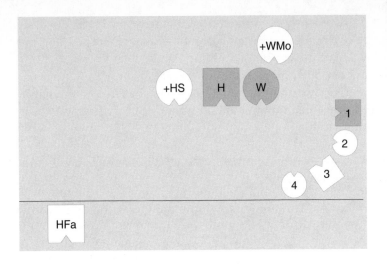

HELLINGER *to wife's representative* How is that for you?

WIFE'S REPRESENTATIVE That's great. Yes, perfect.

HELLINGER *to eldest child* How are you feeling now?

JOSCHA'S REPRESENTATIVE Grandma being here is very good for me.

HELLINGER *to the parents* Take your representatives' places in the constellation and take Joscha with you.

*The parents take their representatives' places. The ill child stands in front of his parents and holds on to his mother.*

HELLINGER *to group* Here we have a picture of the resolution.

*To husband* How do you feel?

HUSBAND I have to get used to it first.

WIFE I feel good.

HELLINGER *to Joscha* How are you doing?

JOSCHA *(loudly)* Good.

HELLINGER *to parents* That's a picture of the resolution. That can be allowed to work in the soul.

*To husband* You have to allow your father to go. He's lost his right to belong.

Okay, let's call him back in.

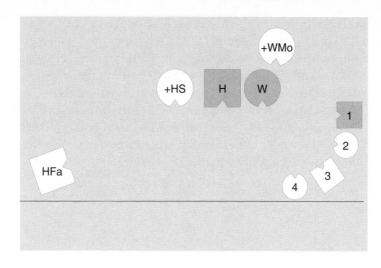

HELLINGER *to husband's father* How was it for you out there?
HUSBAND'S FATHER At first I felt relieved, and then the thing in my chest started up again. But it was good. I had some symptoms.
HELLINGER Look at this picture of the resolution, so you see it too. Okay, that's it.

*To group* This course is very clearly involved with the German past. I've never experienced that anywhere as strongly as in this group.

## IN SERVICE

In my view of the world, I consider each person as he or she is, as someone who has been called into service. I can't explain that, but you can see it. Each person is called into service in some special way, and each person becomes complete only by submitting to this call. Each person, in addition to taking his or her parents, must also take whatever comes in this way. It may be something bad – even the evil are called – and that has far-reaching consequences.

Once a psychiatrist friend of mine said that if you took that seriously, then you'd have to say that Hitler was called into service, too. That would be the consequence of seeing things this way. Any other conclusion would be impossible. For me, it's the only attitude I find that's appropriate, logically justifiable, and philosophically grounded. Then my friend told me that he'd read a book called *My*

*Friend Hitler,* or something like that. It was written by a former room-mate of Hitler's in their youth. He related a story about Hitler going to the opera in Linz and seeing Wagner's *Rienyi der letzte der Tribunen,* and then wandering through the streets of Linz the whole night shouting, "That's my destiny." For him it was unavoidable.

It's the stance I take when I am faced with someone in therapy who is presented as evil or as a criminal. He or she is also called into service, we just don't understand in which way. From this stance I can face and work openly with the whole system.

# Hanna*
## Her father-in-law was in the Gestapo

### Summary

The entanglements: *Hanna's father-in-law was in the Gestapo. Instead of this man being in prison, his son, Hanna's husband, has withdrawn and lives as a recluse in a monastery. Hanna's elder son lives in a similarly isolated and withdrawn manner. Hanna cannot fully take her husband, possibly because he had a prior relationship.*

The resolution: *The husband's father is sent out of the room and the two sons stand with their father. The husband says to his father, "I respect you as my father, and I respect your guilt. I leave the consequences with you. I'm only a child. Please leave me in peace, and my children too. Please." After that the father feels supported and strong.*

*The elder son stands before his father. He says, "Papa, I respect you as my father. I am your son. I'm not allowed to know things about your father. I'll only stay with you."*

*The wife says to her sons, "I entrust you to your father with love."*

HELLINGER *to Hanna* From what you've told me, it seems to me there's something in your present family that needs to be added to what you did yesterday with your family of origin, to complete the picture. So, choose representatives for your present family: your husband, you, and your children. How many children have you got?

HANNA Two. Two sons.

---

* Course in Bremen

103

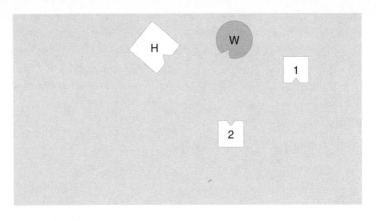

H Husband
**W Wife (Hanna)**
1 First child, a son
2 Second child, a son

HELLINGER *to Hanna (after she has placed the representatives):* Was either of you in a serious relationship before this one, you or your husband?

HANNA No. I suspect, however – and there's some indication that it's true – that my husband had a relationship with a woman, and she was supposed to have been pregnant but didn't want to have the baby. None of that is proven, and I don't know if it has any bearing anyway.

HELLINGER It has a bearing.

HANNA As a matter of principle?

HELLINGER As a matter of principle, I don't talk about things as a matter of principle. What happened to the other woman?

HANNA My husband said she'd gone off to India to care for orphaned children.

HELLINGER This woman?

HANNA Yes. When my husband and I met, I heard that she had gone to India to care for orphans, and that he supposedly hadn't had any contact with her for a long time. That had all happened a few years before we met, and he said he wasn't sure if she'd really been pregnant or if she said that to push him into making a commitment to her.

HELLINGER Of course, that's a very nasty insinuation. *(Hanna nods.)* And what did your husband do, a few years ago?

**104**

HANNA  Up until last year, he was in a monastery for two and a half years – a hermit, so to speak. He said that the family phase was finished for him. He had also wanted to go into a monastery earlier in his life.

HELLINGER  When did he want to go into a monastery?

HANNA  When he was young. After he finished school he went into a Benedictine monastery for about three months.

HELLINGER  Okay, add a representative for this woman.

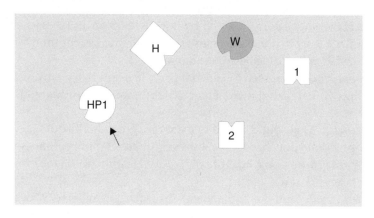

HP1     Husband's first partner

HELLINGER  How is the husband feeling?

HUSBAND  At first I felt very unprotected on my right side, and now I feel a bit crowded.

HELLINGER  What about the wife?

HANNA'S REPRESENTATIVE  I feel pretty much alone. It's really cold over towards my husband. My only connection is to my youngest son.

HELLINGER  How's the elder child feeling?

FIRST CHILD  I feel wrenched around and shoved aside. I don't feel very good. I have no relationships.

HELLINGER  Did anything change when the other woman came in?

FIRST CHILD  Yes, it got more filled up, but I didn't change.

HELLINGER  How's the youngest son doing?

SECOND CHILD  I can feel a very strong love coming from my mother and towards my mother, but I'm standing between my mother and my father. The relationship with my father is relatively weak.

HELLINGER  How's the first partner?

HUSBAND'S FIRST PARTNER  It's nice to look out, but I'd also be interested in what's behind me.

HELLINGER *to Hanna*  Was there something in your husband's original family?

HANNA  My husband's father lost his leg fighting on the front during the war. He was supposed to have been sent to the front as a punishment.

HELLINGER  Why?

HANNA  I think he had something to do with the Nazis and then at the end of the war he didn't want to go along with them and that was the result. At least that used to be my mother-in-law's accusation.

HELLINGER  What did she accuse him of?

HANNA  That he crossed the official party line and that's why he lost his leg, which bound her to an amputee, – unnecessarily, according to her.

HELLINGER  That sounds like a story to me. What did he do?

HANNA  That I don't know. He was in the police, I think perhaps even the Gestapo. So, some kind of police duty. He only was at the front at the very end of the war.

HELLINGER  But not as a punishment, that's hard to imagine. Who was the important person in your constellation yesterday of your family of origin?

HANNA  That was my father's first wife, my brother's mother, who died in childbirth with her second child.

*Hellinger chooses the same representative from the previous day's constellation.*

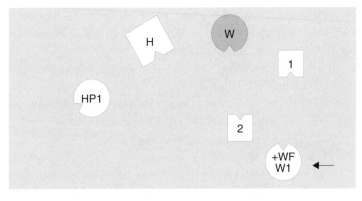

WFW1    Wife's father's first wife

HELLINGER *to younger son* What has changed for you?

SECOND CHILD I feel a certain relationship now from over on the right side, towards the back. It has to do with love.

HELLINGER *to Hanna* My suspicion is that this son is identified with your father's first wife. That would be a cross-gender identification.

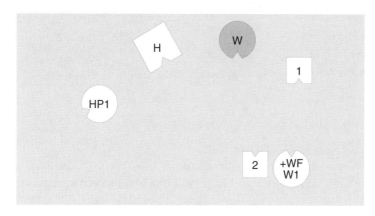

HELLINGER How are you doing there?

SECOND CHILD Just fine.

HELLINGER *to wife's father's first wife* How are you feeling?

WIFE'S FATHER'S FIRST WIFE I've also got a very warm relationship with him.

HELLINGER *to group* That's not a good relationship. It's wrong.

SECOND CHILD Nothing has changed in regards to my mother.

HELLINGER *to mother* Has anything changed for you?

HANNA'S REPRESENTATIVE Yes, I feel somewhat freer.

HELLINGER Exactly.

*To group* If the younger son goes, then she can stay. This boy is endangered.

*To Hanna* In reality, which son is in danger, the younger one or the elder one?

HANNA The elder one is endangered. With the younger one, I really don't know because he is so withdrawn and secretive.

HELLINGER I'll add a representative for the husband's father.

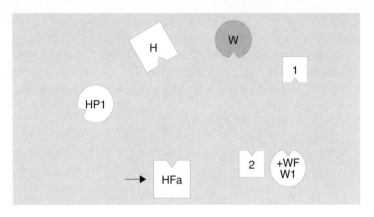

HFa    Husband's father (was in the Gestapo)

HELLINGER *to husband* How is it?

HUSBAND My heart's pounding and it feels good. I wanted to say something to my youngest son. I felt like I had a secret relationship to him that I wasn't acknowledging. I'm only aware of it now that he's standing over there with my wife. I don't have any connection with the other son, I have to keep checking to see if he's really there. Now I'm aware, for the first time, that my father is standing there.

HELLINGER *to eldest son* Is anything different for you?

FIRST CHILD I felt pulled this way and that when the woman came in. On the one hand, I've got someone opposite me, on the other hand, I don't know what significance I have here.

HELLINGER How was it when the grandfather came in?

FIRST CHILD That's good. I'd like to make some contact with him.

*Hellinger changes the positioning.*

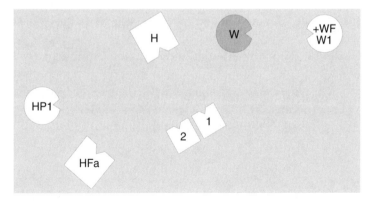

HELLINGER How's that for the husband?

HUSBAND It's wonderful. I can really see that my older son is more important than my younger one. I feel good. My face is cold.

HELLINGER Cold? Can you describe that a bit more?

HUSBAND I've got gooseflesh all over the left side. It feels good.

FIRST CHILD I'm glad to see my father. I'm warm.

SECOND CHILD I feel fairly neutral towards my father. I feel close to my brother on the right.

HELLINGER *to wife* How are you feeling?

HANNA'S REPRESENTATIVE I wanted to say that when my husband's father came in, the coldness on my right side disappeared. Standing here now feels good in a way, but I can't quite get used to not seeing what's going on behind me.

HELLINGER Okay, turn around again.

*To husband's father* I'd like to try something out. Leave the room and close the door behind you.

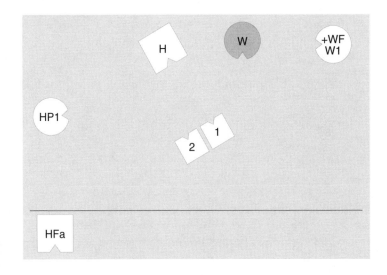

HELLINGER *to husband* What has changed?

HUSBAND What's different for me now is that I only feel right with my two sons. I have no connection to the rest of them.

FIRST CHILD The air's got thinner. It's difficult to breathe.

SECOND CHILD For me it's easier. When he left, my relationship with my father got more intense.

HELLINGER *to group* My suspicion is that the husband's father has lost his right to belong because he was in the Gestapo. That would automatically mean that he committed crimes.

*To Hanna* And does it make sense that your husband is sitting in prison in his father's place, in his monastery? And your elder son?

HANNA *(crying)* Yes. My older son is the most isolated. I think my husband has the strongest connection with him but he rejects the boy because he says they're so much alike.

HELLINGER No, no. If your husband's father doesn't go, then your husband goes. And if your husband doesn't go, then your elder son goes. That's the effect of sympathizing with perpetrators.

*The representative for the husband's father is called back in.*

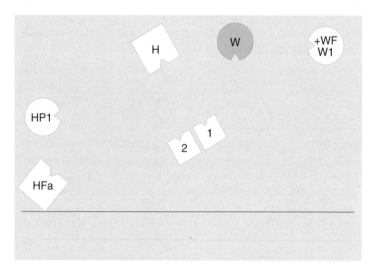

HELLINGER *to husband's father* How did you feel out there?

HUSBAND'S FATHER It was boring. But not so boring that I would have come back into this family.

HELLINGER I've just said here that I suspect the husband's father has lost his right to belong. Instead of the father sitting in prison, his son feels compelled to sit in prison. And if he doesn't disappear on your behalf, then his son is in danger of doing it for him. That seems like the dynamic.

HUSBAND'S FATHER That would fit, because the only feeling I really had was a strong connection to my son. That was all that mattered.

*Hellinger moves the sons next to their father.*

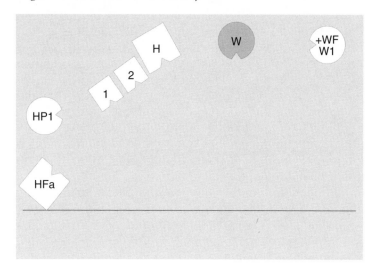

HELLINGER *to husband* Look at your father and tell him, "I respect you as my father."

HUSBAND I respect you as my father.

HELLINGER "And I respect your guilt."

HUSBAND And I respect your guilt.

HELLINGER "I leave you with the consequences."

HUSBAND I leave you with the consequences.

HELLINGER "I'm only a child."

HUSBAND I'm only a child.

HELLINGER "Please, leave me in peace."

HUSBAND Please, leave me in peace.

HELLINGER "And my children, too."

HUSBAND And my children, too. Please.

HELLINGER *to husband's father* How do you feel?

HUSBAND'S FATHER Very straightforward and supported.

HELLINGER Exactly.

HUSBAND'S FATHER I feel very powerful now.

HELLINGER Exactly. When someone is left with their own guilt, it's a form of respect and the person regains stature.

*To elder son* How are you?

FIRST CHILD I feel some life coming into me and I can breathe out, but it's still difficult.

111

HELLINGER Stand in front of your father and look at him.

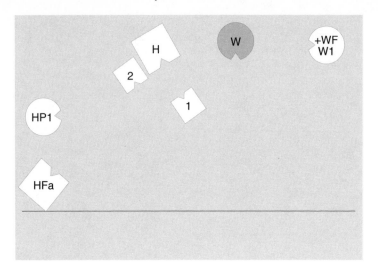

HELLINGER Say, "Papa."
FIRST CHILD Papa
HELLINGER "I respect you as my father."
FIRST CHILD I respect you as my father
HELLINGER "And I'm your son."
FIRST CHILD And I'm your son.
HELLINGER "I'm not allowed to know things about your father."
FIRST CHILD I'm not allowed to know things about your father.
HELLINGER "I'll only stay with you."
FIRST CHILD I'll only stay with you.
HELLINGER *to husband* How is that?
HUSBAND I'm free. It feels free.

*Hellinger puts the two sons opposite their father again and sends the husband's father back out of the room.*

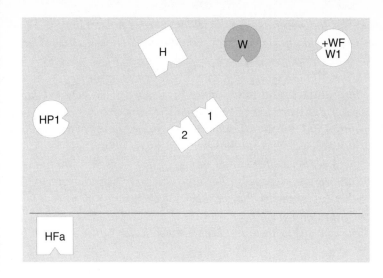

HELLINGER *to wife* How are you?
HANNA'S REPRESENTATIVE I also feel freer.

*Hellinger moves her closer to her husband.*

HANNA'S REPRESENTATIVE I felt better a bit further away.

*She moves back to her original place. Hellinger brings Hanna into the constellation to replace her representative.*

HELLINGER *to Hanna* Tell your sons, "I entrust you to your father."
HANNA I entrust you to your father. *(She weeps.)*
HELLINGER "With love."
HANNA *(very moved)* With love. And I love you.
HELLINGER "But still, I entrust you to your father."
HANNA But still, I entrust you to your father.
HELLINGER "With love."
HANNA With love.
HELLINGER Okay, that's it.

## SUMMARY

The entanglements: *Hanna's father-in-law was in the Gestapo. Instead of him being in prison, his son has withdrawn and lives as a recluse in a mon-*

*astery. Hanna's elder son has also withdrawn and isolated himself. Hanna does not dare to take her husband, probably because he had a prior relationship.*

The resolution: *The husband's father was sent out of the room and the two sons stood with their father. The husband said to his father, "I respect you as my father, and I respect your guilt. I leave the consequences with you. I'm only a child. Please leave me in peace, and my children too. Please." After that the father felt supported and strong.*

*The elder son stood before his father. He said, "Papa, I respect you as my father. I am your son. I'm not allowed to know things about your father. I'll only stay with you."*

*The wife said to her sons, "I entrust you to your father with love."*

## THE ORDER

HELLINGER *to group* Are there any questions?

QUESTION The son said, "I'm not allowed to know things about your father." Often there are family secrets that are important for the family, and I'd like to know if I should keep them to myself or what I should do with it. Is it better to tell my children or to keep it to myself?

HELLINGER Do you know what the purpose of writing history is? It's a propagation of evil. Yes. Because what's past is not allowed to be past. Still, your question is important.

Okay, it's clear that he was in the Gestapo, so there's no point in keeping that a secret. What he did or didn't do is none of the children's business. Children aren't allowed to get involved in these things. If they did, they would become the secret judges of their parents and would punish themselves terribly for that. That goes against the natural order. The parents' guilt has nothing to do with the children.

It's difficult for children to stay out of it because they may secretly want to carry the guilt for their parents. But that's hubris and can only lead to tragedy. That's a presumption on the part of a child who, despite a secondary position, believes that he or she can do something good, even against the order of things. It is always doomed to failure, if not with the child, then with his or her children. You have to look at it over several generations, then you can see what the effect is.

**114**

The intimate relationship between parents is none of their children's business. If a child is told details about his or her parents' relationship, it has a bad effect on the child. The solution for the child is to forget it. It's a discipline at a high level, this forgetting – a kind of withdrawal and deep centering. Then it's gone.

QUESTION I'm shocked to hear you say that the parents' guilt is none of their children's business. Do you mean only regarding intimate issues and intimate guilt, or does that apply to others things as well, things that are public, or out in the open? When I think of all the memorials and commemorations that we've experienced recently – today there's another one of those – where we talk, not about the guilt of the descendants, but about their shame; does that apply here as well? Shame implies guilt, or at least a participation in the guilt. Is what you're saying true of these public issues? I've been one of those who say that remembering will prevent recurrence; is that completely off base?

HELLINGER The ancient philosophers had a private area – an Arkanum – which was reserved for themselves. Outsiders were not allowed in. I also have an Arkanum where I keep things to myself. These things I don't say.

PARTICIPANT I can understand that for the personal things that I don't tell my children. I don't need to tell my children or my grandchildren what my father did in Stalingrad or something. That's clear. I can keep that to myself and not say anything. I forgave my father for that on his deathbed. That's cleared.

HELLINGER How terrible! A child forgiving his father!

PARTICIPANT Yes, because I had suffered from that. Then, there was no other alternative. Then. Today perhaps it would be different. But really, back to the question; is it really wrong what we're doing in trying to keep awareness alive of the guilt of what happened?

HELLINGER I ask myself the same thing. As far as forgiveness goes, the saying is: What I forgive, I pack in my own rucksack.

PARTICIPANT Yes, I've noticed. That, I have noticed.

HELLINGER Exactly.

PARTICIPANT But I've been able to put down the rucksack in the meantime.

HELLINGER Your comments show that you haven't done that.

PARTICIPANT Okay, I'll give it some more thought.

HELLINGER Okay.

QUESTION Are there differences between the different generations? I noticed that you said something different to the grandchild about what he was allowed to know than you said to the son.

HELLINGER I held to the order of things exactly. The son speaks to his father and the father speaks to his father, but the grandchild doesn't speak to the grandfather. I held the hierarchy exactly. As far as I could see, that had a good effect.

*To representative of the elder son* How was that?

REPRESENTATIVE Yes, it was a relief. It felt good.

HELLINGER *to group* Otherwise he would have got mixed up in things between his father and his grandfather.

QUESTION You said, "has lost his right to belong." Up until now I've only heard that when some member of the system has committed a crime such as giving a child away, or something like that. But in this case it was different because he had presumably committed crimes which did not directly have to do with the family.

HELLINGER Murder always leads to being excluded from your own system, not only the murder of another member of the system. There is no reparation for murder. It's different, for example, if a woman gives her child away. Then, she has, as a rule, lost her rights and has no claim to her child, but she hasn't lost her place in the system. That's also something that can sometimes be atoned for. For example, the woman could seek out the child later and say, "I have done you an injustice and I'm sorry. Now you have a place in my heart as my child." She can't ask the child for forgiveness, that would be bad for the child. Parents can't lower themselves to their children, that's a basic principle. And children can't put themselves above their parents, for example to forgive them. That goes against the order and doesn't work.

# Mirjam*

## Her grandmother was a survivor of Theresienstadt, and four of the grandmother's siblings died.

### SUMMARY

The entanglements: *Mirjam's Jewish grandmother survived Theresien-stadt, but four of her brothers and sisters were killed. The mother has broken off all contact with her Jewish relatives. Mirjam had an elder sister who died at the age of three.*

The resolution: *The grandmother and her dead siblings are brought into the constellation. The grandmother bows down before her dead brothers and sisters and tells them, "I carry you in my heart."*

*The mother also bows before the dead and before her mother, but cannot reach them.*

*The father takes Mirjam by the hand and goes with her to her grand-mother and the dead and with her, bows down before them. Mirjam embraces her grandmother, sobbing, as well as her dead great-aunt. She says, "Dear Aunt, you are still here in me." Then she approaches her dead sister, looks at her and says, "Dear Sister." The sisters embrace.*

*As the mother remains cold, she is placed with the dead. There, her pain breaks through with tears. She says, "That's it."*

MIRJAM  I have a question. Half of my family is Jewish and fourteen years ago I gave birth to a severely disabled son. Could there be any connection?

HELLINGER  No. You have to claim your fate that you have a disabled son, and accept it as your fate. It's a great challenge and something special.

* Course in Bremen

117

MIRJAM  Yes, that it is.

HELLINGER  You can feel that, and I can see it.

MIRJAM  But there's no connection to the Jewish family members who were killed …

HELLINGER  No. I would see the two things separately. But Jewish families, or half-Jewish families, have a heavy fate because the dead continue to have an effect. The evil is not past and cannot be past.

MIRJAM  I don't understand. Would you work with me later?

HELLINGER  I'll do it immediately. Come here. Are you married?

MIRJAM  I'm not married. I had my son with a man that I lived with. I currently have a very close relationship with a man who is married and who lives with his children. My problem, as best I can describe it, is that I can't handle these constant goodbyes. I fall into a kind of despair.

HELLINGER  What was the situation in your family of origin?

MIRJAM  My mother is half Jewish. She wasn't allowed to marry my father because he's Aryan. They had a child, a daughter who died at age three. When the war was over, they married. Then my mother had a lot of miscarriages, five I think. In the meantime, my father had left her. She wanted to save the marriage and managed to have me. I didn't save the marriage, and they got a divorce. My father kidnapped me and I was locked up with some people, but my mother searched for me and took me back. My mother then married another man, and I grew up with him. He died when I was fifteen. I have a very close relationship with my mother. She's still alive at 85.

HELLINGER  What about her relatives?

MIRJAM  My mother despised my Jewish grandmother *(sighs)* and they lived in conflict and hate. My mother is a latent anti-Semitic. I don't know how to explain that. It was difficult for her with her mother.

HELLINGER  I can tell you how to explain that. She never fully gave thanks for her survival.

MIRJAM  Perhaps …

HELLINGER  Why perhaps? She didn't give thanks.

MIRJAM  I say perhaps because she's a wise and very positive person. She's not bitter and she's emerged from her difficult life with strength.

HELLINGER  Which of her relatives died?

MIRJAM  Her aunts and uncles. My grandmother had four siblings, or five, and they all died.

HELLINGER How did your grandmother survive?

MIRJAM She was in Theresienstadt, and then was liberated.

HELLINGER She certainly didn't give thanks. Okay, we'll set up your family of origin: your father, your mother, you, and the child that died.

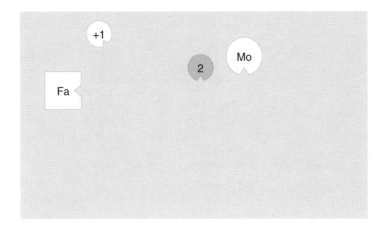

Fa Father
Mo Mother
1    First child, a daughter (died at the age of 3)
**2    Second child, a daughter (Mirjam)**

HELLINGER *to father* How do you feel?

FATHER I feel isolated and I feel drawn over there *(indicates in the direction of his wife and younger daughter).*

HELLINGER Where exactly?

FATHER More towards my wife, but I see the two of them as one unit.

HELLINGER *to mother* How are you feeling?

MOTHER I feel much the same. I also thought, "Where's my husband?" I'm looking forward and the space is nice. I'm very close to my daughter, but somehow not all that close. Something's not right.

HELLINGER *to deceased child* How are you?

FIRST CHILD I'm very well. I feel just fine here.

HELLINGER *to Mirjam's representative* How do you feel?

MIRJAM'S REPRESENTATIVE I'm not so fine. I notice that I haven't got any connection to my father, I don't know him at all. And my mother is very powerful, so much so that she almost overwhelms me. I have a yearning for my dead sister.

HELLINGER *to Mirjam* Now add representatives for your grandmother and her siblings who were killed. How many were there?

MIRJAM Four or five. But we have no contact. My mother broke off all contact with her Jewish relatives, except for her brother because he's an outsider, too.

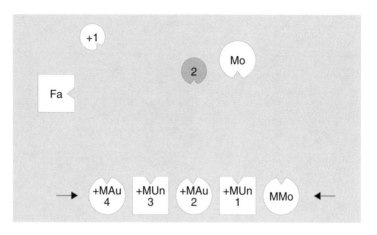

MMo   Mother's mother (survived Theresienstadt)
MUn   Mother's uncles (died)
MAu   Mother's aunts (died)

HELLINGER *to mother* How is it now?

MOTHER I feel terrible. Oh, I could kill them. I don't want to see them, I don't want to see them at all. They'll be the death of me.

HELLINGER *to Mirjam's representative* How are you now?

MIRJAM'S REPRESENTATIVE Also not good. What's there is massive and I feel very threatened.

HELLINGER *to grandmother* How are you feeling?

GRANDMOTHER I feel fine. I feel strong and I've got a connection to my daughter and granddaughter. I don't mind that they said all those negative things, I've got a good feeling towards them.

MOTHER'S FIRST UNCLE It's okay. To the right it's very cold. Otherwise, I'm just looking at all this.

MOTHER'S SECOND AUNT It's nice. I feel very secure.

MOTHER'S THIRD UNCLE As my sister's daughter said that, I was very touched. Then, I discovered I'm dead. I'm not there.

MOTHER'S FOURTH AUNT I can't look at any of them. My knees are weak, as though I'm going to collapse.

120

FATHER  I'm not getting anything from my wife. I'm just looking at them over there and I would really like to run away, but I don't dare run away. It's as if I were rooted to my place.

HELLINGER  That's too powerful.

GRANDMOTHER  I feel almost triumphant here, very powerful.

HELLINGER *to grandmother*  Go and stand in front of your dead brothers and sisters. Go from one to the other and bow before them, with respect.

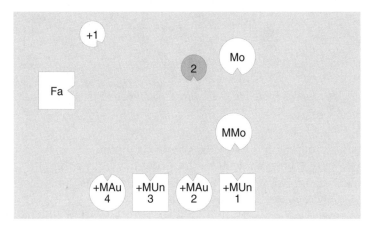

*The grandmother moves slowly from one to the next bowing before them. They are very touched.*

HELLINGER to grandmother  Now say to them all, "I carry you in my heart."

GRANDMOTHER  I carry you in my heart.

HELLINGER  Now stand next to them again.

*To mother*  How are you feeling now?

MOTHER  With each bow I felt a bit more relieved. I can look at them now, there's no threat there anymore.

HELLINGER  Now you do the same thing. Go to each one and bow before them. Start with the dead aunts and uncles and then go to your mother.

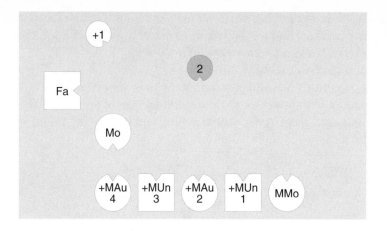

*The mother moves from one to the other, bowing, and then returns to her place.*

HELLINGER *to grandmother* How was that for you?
GRANDMOTHER I had some difficulty. I couldn't really accept it.
HELLINGER She didn't really do it fully. Her heart wasn't in it.
*To Mirjam's representative* How are you doing?
MIRJAM'S REPRESENTATIVE Nothing much has changed. At the beginning I felt a little relieved, and as my grandmother bowed down to her brothers and sisters, I felt something like joy. As my mother did the same thing, I was really happy at first, but then ... *(she shakes her head.)*
HELLINGER Precisely.

*Hellinger puts Mirjam in the constellation in place of her representative.*

HELLINGER *to father* Now take your daughter by the hand and bow down with her in front of each of them. Begin with the grandmother.

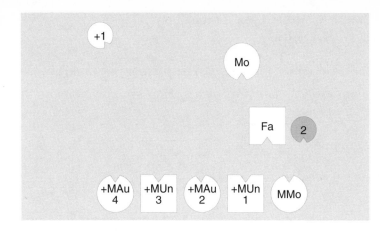

As Mirjam bows before her grandmother, she is very moved and covers her face with her hands and weeps.

HELLINGER Go to your grandmother.

Mirjam embraces her grandmother, sobbing. Then she strokes her grandmother's head and smiles at her. She leaves, but then returns once more and the two of them hold hands and smile at one another. Mirjam bows deeply once again and then goes with her father to the dead relatives, looks at each one and bows deeply. With the eldest great-aunt, she lays her hands on her shoulders and says, "Dear Aunt, you are still here in me." Then she embraces the younger great-aunt.

Hellinger moves the father next to his dead daughter and brings Mirjam to them.

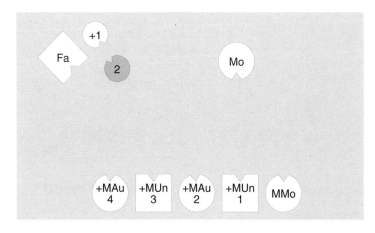

HELLINGER *to Mirjam* Look at her and say, "Dear Sister."
MIRJAM Dear Sister.

*Mirjam embraces her sister tenderly. Then she stands next to her father.*

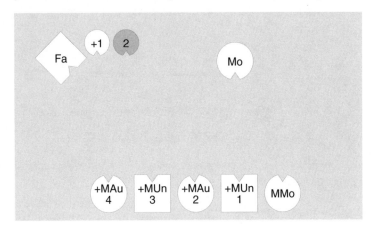

HELLINGER *to mother* How are you doing?
MOTHER A bit better. I see that it's good that they're doing this. I can't really do it. When the grandma did that, it was also good. But I don't have any feelings myself.
HELLINGER Go and stand next to the ones who have died.

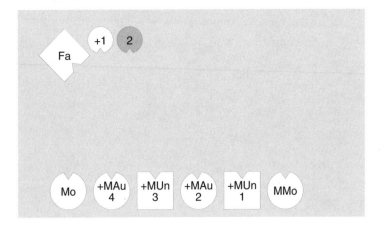

*As she stands there, she begins to sob aloud and says, "That's it."*

HELLINGER Exactly.

*To group* Okay, I think we've shown what reconciliation really is, and that it only comes through pain. Not because of memorials or com- memorations, or accusations. Okay, that was it.

## EXCLUDED PERPETRATORS WILL BE REPRESENTED

What I have observed in the course of my work is that victims can find peace only when they are able to give the perpetrators a place next to themselves. Perpetrators find peace when they lie down next to their victims and are taken in there. In a system where the perpe- trator is not looked at and taken in, a child usually represents the missing perpetrator, and exhibits attitudes and energies similar to those of the perpetrator. If you know this, it's easier to understand the feelings of Mirjam's mother. She is probably representing the despised perpetrator. This is why she felt better standing next to the victims.

## DIFFERENTIATING FEELINGS

HELLINGER *to group* I want to say something about different feelings. The resistance to bowing down, which we saw with the mother and at first with the grandmother, was a defence against the pain and against the thankfulness for their own survival. It was clear with both of them. Then I had to look for a way to break through the first feel- ings, for example, when the grandmother felt so powerful at first.

*To grandmother's representative* How quickly that changed and how soothing for the soul when the appropriate feelings came out.

*To mother's representative* The pain that came out for you later, when you stood beside the dead, that was a primary feeling.

*To group* A primary feeling is a feeling that is appropriate to the situ- ation, and a feeling that connects. You have seen how the representa- tives who had primary feelings could open their eyes and that the feelings made connections.

*To Mirjam* You demonstrated beautifully how the love could flow when you looked at each one with your eyes open and could feel the connections.

125

*To group* That's an important criterion for primary feelings the eyes are open. With primary feelings I'm in contact. When someone grieves with primary grief, they look at the person for whom they're grieving. The pain is experienced in the view of the other person. In defensive grief, the person closes their eyes. These feelings are fed by fantasy, and to have them you have to close your eyes.

To come back to the subject of memorials; who is being looked at in these memorials? Mostly it's the perpetrators and seldom the victims. In front of the victims, we close our eyes. That's why it produces little pain or empathy with the victims.

For primary feelings the eyes must be open. Primary feelings allow you to empathize without being pulled in. You can feel with but at the same time remain collected in yourself. You don't feel threatened or trapped by it. You can feel, but with freedom. That's another important criterion for primary feelings. On the other hand, in the presence of secondary feelings, you don't feel free. Through secondary feelings, a person often induces others to act instead of acting themselves. So, those are two kinds of feelings, primary and secondary – or defensive.

The third kind of feelings are those that are taken over from another person. Then it's important to see the other person from whom the feeling has been taken over. For example, when someone feels in the right, in a superior way, it's a feeling taken over from someone else. One who feels as though they have to save the world has feelings taken over from someone else. Those who feel righteous or who fight for a cause are experiencing feelings taken over from someone else.

Then there is another feeling that is on a higher level – a meta-feeling. These feelings are without emotion, they are pure strength. A therapist has to remain in the sphere of meta-feelings, as in the constellation we've just seen. That came very close to me and I had to stay on the level of meta-feelings in order to be able to act. Then I can keep everything in view.

Okay, so much for the different kinds of feelings. Are there any other questions?

QUESTION What about outrage towards perpetrators and the attempt to prevent repetitions in the future with warnings and remembering?

HELLINGER There's a resistance to changing one's basic view of this outrage over perpetrators and remembering, and it's often connected to the fact that, identifying with the victims allows one to feel better, superior, and critical. That way, you're spared your own suffering, or looking into your own depth, your own temptations, and your own experiences of failure. Those who feel outrage presume they have more rights than others and feel superior, exactly as the perpetrators felt. But when I identify with someone, that person is no longer visible to me. By identifying with him or her, I avoid looking him in the eye. Whoever looks the dead in the eye can't carry on with a sense of outrage or presume to take over that which is the right of the dead.

# Heinrich*
## His mother slit her wrists and those of her four children

### SUMMARY

The entanglements: *Heinrich's mother slit her wrists and those of her children. This occurred at the end of the war after she had been raped countless times by Russian soldiers. Another woman who had also planned to kill herself and her children stopped after killing her youngest child and was able to rescue the others. Heinrich's mother's father poisoned himself. The murders probably began with him. Heinrich is identified with him and is worried that he, too, may be dangerous to others.*

The resolution: *The grandfather is sent from the room. The mother bows before the other woman and says, "Thank you. I accept this from you, even at the price of the dead child."*

*Then the father, who was in a prisoner of war camp at the time, is placed next to the mother. Heinrich says to him. "It's good that you're here again. At last." Heinrich goes to his father and embraces him, weeping.*

*Heinrich tells his son, who is also present, "Your great-grandfather is a murderer and he has to go. You have to let him go out of your heart, just as I'm letting him go out of my heart. And you come to me." Heinrich embraces his son and says to him, "I'll hold you and keep you alive, my son."*

HELLINGER *to Heinrich* What's the issue?
HEINRICH There was something that happened that was very drastic. In 1945, my mother slit her wrists as well as mine and those of my brothers. I've dealt with that for myself, but I'm worried that I'll pass this on to my wife and children.

* Course in Magdeburg

128

HELLINGER How many children were there?

HEINRICH Four brothers.

HELLINGER And all four of you had your wrists slit?

HEINRICH Yes.

HELLINGER Why did she do this in 1945?

HELLINGER My father was missing, and she was certain that he was dead. And she had been raped countless times when the Russians came.

HELLINGER That's relevant, of course. We'll set up your family of origin: your mother and the four children. We'll add a representative for your father later.

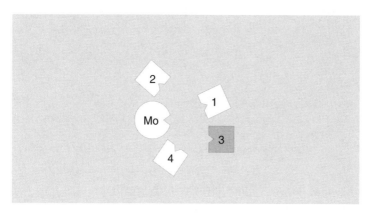

Mo  Mother
1   First child, a son
2   Second child, a son
**3   Third child, a son (Heinrich)**
4   Fourth child, a son

HELLINGER Did you all survive?

HEINRICH We all survived except for my mother's father. He was also involved and he took poison. He was a pharmacist.

HELLINGER Who initiated the whole thing?

HEINRICH I think it was most likely my mother, but with consultation.

HELLINGER How were you saved?

HEINRICH Through a woman who lived with us, who also had four children. She had been planning to do the same thing and had already killed her youngest child when she lost her nerve and rescued us.

HELLINGER  Add a representative for your grandfather and also one for the woman and for the child she killed.

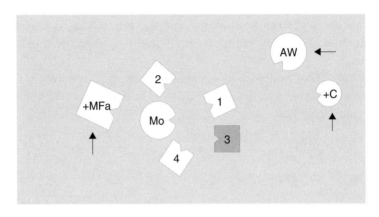

MFa  Mother's father, who killed himself with poison
AW  Another woman, who killed her youngest child and then rescued the others
C  Child of this woman, a daughter, who was killed by her mother

HELLINGER *to mother's father*  How is it for you?
MOTHER'S FATHER *(clutching his head)*  Everything is open up on top and I have a tendency to fall over.
HELLINGER  You have to leave. Leave the room and close the door behind you.

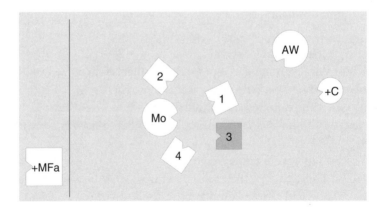

HELLINGER *to group* He's the guilty one. He has to leave the system. He's the actual murderer.

*To mother* How's the mother?

MOTHER I feel a bit better now. When he placed the representatives for my sons, I couldn't look at any of them. He smiled when he did that, and I couldn't stand it. I couldn't stand my sons, either. When the grandfather came in, *(she sighs)* I can't even describe it. It was unbearable. I got very hot and had the feeling that I was swaying backwards and forwards. I couldn't stand still.

HELLINGER *to eldest son* How are you doing?

FIRST CHILD I have a heavy burden on my shoulders. I feel like a water bearer. It got lighter when my grandfather left.

SECOND CHILD I've got a pressure on my chest and I can hardly breathe or swallow here.

HEINRICH'S REPRESENTATIVE I'm feeling waves of anxiety and grief. When my grandfather came in, I panicked, and I saw that in his face, too. Once he was outside, I felt really happy. It's a lot better now.

FOURTH CHILD When my grandfather was there, my heart was pounding. Now, I've got the feeling that I could fall over forwards – not into my eldest brother's arms – rather, to the floor. He's the only one I can see. I'm barely aware of the others.

MOTHER I'm feeling better. My heart was pounding and now I can look at the two sons in front of me.

*Hellinger places all four sons opposite the mother. He moves the other woman and her dead child next to the mother.*

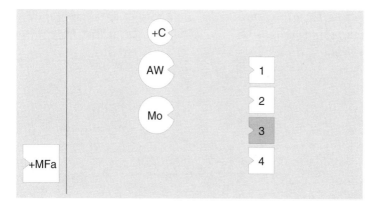

HELLINGER *to mother* What is it?

MOTHER I want to get out of here. When my sons were standing in front of me, I already had the feeling I had to step back. Now that the other woman has come, I want to get away backwards to the right.

HELLINGER Stand in front of the other woman.

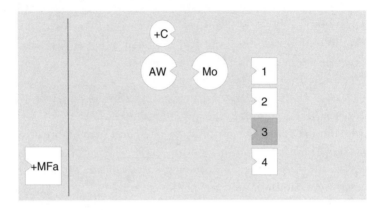

HELLINGER *to mother* Bow down deeply before her. Then, straighten up again and say to her, "Thank you."

MOTHER Thank you.

HELLINGER "I accept this from you."

MOTHER I accept this from you.

HELLINGER "Even at the price of the dead child."

MOTHER Even at the price of the dead child. Thank you.

HELLINGER Stand next to her and put your arm around her.

*The mother stands next to the other woman and they put their arms around each other. Up to this point, the dead child has only been staring at the floor. Hellinger straightens the child up and asks the woman to put her arm around this child.*

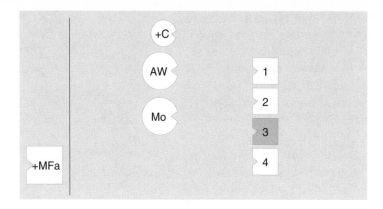

HELLINGER How is that for the mother now?

MOTHER Liberating.

HELLINGER Exactly. You hadn't really taken your rescue from her.

*To eldest son* How are you feeling now?

FIRST CHILD This is nice, it's good.

SECOND CHILD Standing here, I felt better. Then, when I heard what my mother said, I started having trouble breathing again. Now, it's better again.

HEINRICH'S REPRESENTATIVE My anxiety is gone.

FOURTH CHILD I feel lighter.

*Hellinger chooses a representative for the father and places him next to the mother.*

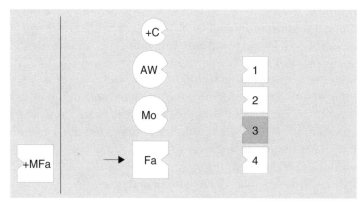

Fa Father

HELLINGER  How is that?

MOTHER  It's good. There's a protection.

FATHER  I feel good here.

FIRST CHILD  I feel more complete now.

SECOND CHILD  It's okay.

HEINRICH'S REPRESENTATIVE  I feel relieved of a burden.

FOURTH CHILD  I don't see only my mother, I can see my father now, too. That's better.

HELLINGER *to Heinrich*  Take your place in the constellation. Tell your father, "It's good that you're here again."

HEINRICH  It's good that you're here again.

HELLINGER  "At last."

HEINRICH  At last.

HELLINGER  Go to him.

*Heinrich moves to his father and they embrace warmly. Heinrich is very touched and cries.*

HELLINGER *(after a pause) to Heinrich*  Go back to your place. I want to tell you something. This woman and all of her children belong to your family. What happened to her husband, did he come back?

HEINRICH  She was already separated from her husband at the time she lived with us.

HELLINGER  How many other children did she have?

HEINRICH  Three sons besides the little girl.

HELLINGER  They all belong to this family, and you have to take them as your siblings. And you have to care for them like siblings. Is that clear?

HEINRICH  I understand that. I've also felt something like that.

HELLINGER  Okay. I want to tell you something else. You are identified with your grandfather. You're identified with the murderer. That's why you're worried that you could kill someone.

*To group*  That is because the guilt hasn't been left with the grandfather.

*To Heinrich*  He must be let go out of the system, as someone who has lost his right to belong. You have to say to him, "You must go and I'll stay with my father." Is that clear to you?

HEINRICH  I've said the opposite.

HELLINGER  Precisely. That's why you're in danger.

*Hellinger calls the grandfather's representative back in.*

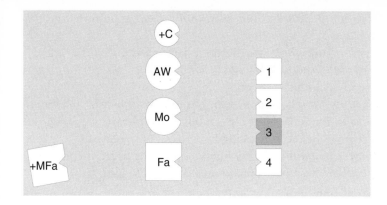

HELLINGER How did you feel out there?

MOTHER'S FATHER I had halfway got over the craziness – because it was crazy, it was like I was possessed – and then, I met his actual son, who was also out in the hallway.

HELLINGER God.

HEINRICH'S SON He came out there and we talked.

HELLINGER That's macabre.

HEINRICH I don't understand.

HELLINGER He met your son out there.

HEINRICH I sent him out, because I thought it would be better.

*Hellinger calls the son and places him in the constellation.*

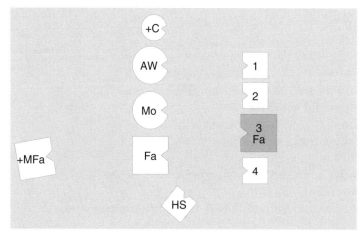

HS Heinrich's son

HELLINGER *to Heinrich*  Tell him, "Your great-grandfather is a murderer."

HEINRICH  Your great-grandfather is a murderer.

HELLINGER  "And he has to go."

HEINRICH  And he has to go.

HELLINGER  "You have to let him go out of your heart." Tell him that.

HEINRICH  You have to let him go out of your heart.

HELLINGER  "Just as I'm letting him go out of my heart."

HEINRICH  Just as I'm letting him go out of my heart.

HELLINGER  "And you come to me." Say that to him.

HEINRICH  And you come to me.

HELLINGER *to son*  Go to your father.

*Heinrich's son goes to his father, who embraces him and holds him tightly.*

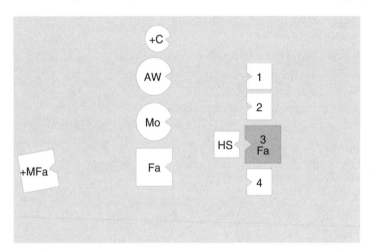

HELLINGER *to Heinrich*  Tell him, "I'll hold you."

HEINRICH  I'll hold you.

HELLINGER  "And keep you alive."

HEINRICH  And keep you alive.

*Heinrich is very moved and says to his son, "My son."*

HELLINGER *to Heinrich*  Resist the weakness and find your inner strength.

HELLINGER *to son*  Okay, how are you now?

**136**

HEINRICH'S SON  Yeah, I'm okay.

HELLINGER  Your father will have to tell you about what all that was about.

*To Heinrich*  That's all.

# Grace*
## Her grandparents and ten aunts and uncles were murdered

### SUMMARY

The entanglements: *Grace's parents were able to escape to Asia and came to Germany after the war. Grace grew up in Germany. Her eldest brother died one day after his birth. Her grandparents and ten aunts and uncles were murdered.*

The resolution: *Grace's father takes her by the hand and with her bows to each of his parents and siblings. Then, her mother takes her by the hand and with her bows to each of her parents and siblings. Grace says to her grandparents, "Please look kindly on me. Look, I am still alive. I take my life as a gift and I give you a place in my heart. In me, you are still here. Please bless me when I live on, even though you are dead." She embraces her deceased grandparents, aunts, and uncles.*

Following that, she turns to her dead brother and embraces him saying, "I have missed you very much." She takes her place between her parents, where she feels secure and protected.

HELLINGER  What do you want to work on?

GRACE  Just my history and the way it unfolds in my present life. I'm a child of Holocaust survivors and I think this marks my life. The second thing that marks my life is that I also grew up in Germany after the war.

HELLINGER  You grew up in Germany after the war?

GRACE  Yes. The way I see it working in my life is in the total absence of relationships.

HELLINGER  How did your parents survive?

---

* Course in London (1)

138

GRACE My parents were in Asia. My parents were Polish Jews who escaped to Asia. I was born at the end of the war. So after the war, they just got stuck as displaced persons in Germany, and I just ended up by chance becoming a German.

HELLINGER Any relatives who died?

GRACE All of them, practically, except my parents and a sister of my father's who survived.

HELLINGER Now just name those who died.

GRACE I should name them? I couldn't. I don't know their names.

HELLINGER I mean your grandfather, grandparents.

GRACE All the grandparents.

HELLINGER The four grandparents died?

GRACE Yes.

HELLINGER Who else?

GRACE Everyone. My mother had four sisters and a brother and they all perished. My father was one of seven children and he took out his sister and everyone else perished. Both of my parents were the youngest which means the rest of the family had children already. They weren't married, my parents weren't married when the war broke out. It's just huge. I can't distinguish anymore.

HELLINGER I will select the representatives.

GRACE Maybe I should say one more thing. My father always told me, both of my parents told me, that I look like one of his sisters.

HELLINGER You should actually. We'll choose representatives for your grandparents and for all your uncles and aunts who perished. Have you got any brothers and sisters?

GRACE I have a sister and two brothers, but one of my brothers died when he was just a day old. I'm the first, but I actually shouldn't be the first one. Actually, I'm the second one.

HELLINGER The first one died?

GRACE Yes.

HELLINGER We need him too. Choose representatives for all those who perished, your father's family and your mother's family.

*Grace chooses representatives.*

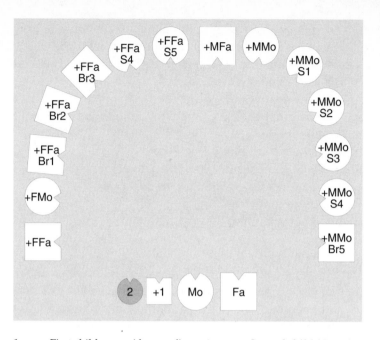

| 1 | First child, a son (deceased) | **2** | **Second child (Grace)** |
|---|---|---|---|
| Fa | Father | Mo | Mother |
| PGFa | Father's father | MGMo | Mother's mother |
| PGMo | Father's mother | MGFa | Mother's father |
| FaBr1 | Father's first brother | MoS1 | Mother's first sister |
| FaBr2 | Father's second brother | MoS2 | Mother's second sister |
| FaBr3 | Father's third brother | MoS3 | Mother's third sister |
| FaS4 | Father's first sister | MoS4 | Mother's fourth sister |
| FaS5 | Father's second sister | MoBr5 | Mother's brother |

HELLINGER *to Grace* Now look at them, at each one of them.
*To father* Now take her by the hand and go with her to everybody in your family, and bow in respect before everybody.

*Grace and father bow deeply in front of paternal grandfather.*

HELLINGER *to Grace* There's no hurry, take the full time necessary. *(Long silence)* Look at him and say, "Dear grandpa, ... " *(Grace begins to weep.)*
GRACE Dear grandpa, ...
HELLINGER "look at me ... "
GRACE *(still weeping)* Look at me ...
HELLINGER "Kindly."

GRACE  Kindly.

HELLINGER  "I'm still alive."

GRACE  I'm still alive.

HELLINGER  And tell him, "I take my life as a special gift."

GRACE  I take my life as a special gift.

HELLINGER  "In my heart you are alive."

GRACE  In my heart you are alive. *Grace and paternal grandfather embrace.*

HELLINGER *to Grace* Breathe deeply. *(Long pause)*

*To* FATHER  Then take her to her grandmother and do the same.

Grace and father bow deeply in front of paternal grandmother.

HELLINGER  Say, "Dear grandmother, … "

GRACE  Dear grandmother, … *(weeping)*

HELLINGER  "I honour you."

GRACE  I honour you.

HELLINGER  "Please be friendly while I'm alive and you are dead."

GRACE  Please be friendly while I'm alive and you are dead.

HELLINGER  Go to her. *Grace and paternal grandmother embrace.* Then you go on and bow in front of each of them with respect and love. *Grace and her father bow deeply in front of each paternal uncle and aunt.*

*To mother* Now you take her by the hand and go to your parents and brothers and sisters. Just bow deeply. *Grace bows deeply in front of her maternal grandfather and they embrace.*

*To Grace* Ask him for his blessing.

GRACE *(sobbing quietly)* Please bless me.

HELLINGER  Say, "In my heart you have a place."

GRACE  In my heart you have a place.

HELLINGER  "In me you are still alive."

GRACE  In me you are still alive.

HELLINGER *to Grace* Now move on to your grandmother. *Grace and maternal grandmother embrace, then Grace and mother bow in front of and embrace each maternal aunt and uncle.* Now embrace your brother. *She embraces her deceased brother.* Now I'll place you between your parents.

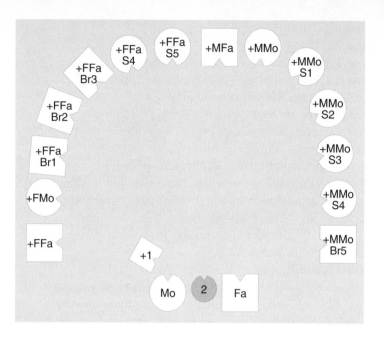

HELLINGER  Look at your father and look at your mother. How are you feeling?

GRACE  I feel secure now. I feel safe. I wanted to say something to my brother.

HELLINGER  Yes do.

GRACE *to brother*  You took the easy way out.

HELLINGER *to Grace*  Tell him, "I missed you."

GRACE *(tearfully)*  I missed you.

HELLINGER  "You are my big brother."

GRACE  You are my big brother.

HELLINGER  "I'm your little sister."

GRACE  I'm your little sister.

HELLINGER *to representatives*  I just want to ask you what your experience was?

PATERNAL GRANDFATHER  Very sad and moved and yet very happy and glad that she is alive.

PATERNAL GRANDMOTHER  I felt very happy and felt, "You silly girl, go and live your life and don't worry about us."

FATHER'S ELDEST BROTHER  I felt very sad and moved and very warm towards her and was wishing her well.

142

Father's Second Brother  I felt very sad and I felt my heart open to you.

Father's Third Brother  I felt very sad and a lot of shivering all over, an engine moving. *(Pause)* There was a point where it felt like standing in front of a firing squad as well.

Father's Eldest Sister  I felt deeply moved and very glad to have the opportunity to meet you, and to know that you are alive.

Father's Second Sister  I felt very sad and wanted you to live.

Maternal Grandfather  Very moved, joy and sorrow simultaneously, and proud.

Maternal Grandmother  I felt very sad and then very proud, and then very hot when we hugged.

Mother's Eldest Sister  I felt very shivery, tingly, full of excitement at meeting you.

Mother's Second Sister  My heart really hurt, and then I was very glad to embrace you.

Mother's Third Sister  I felt very full-hearted and full of love and full of hope for you to be truly alive.

Mother's Fourth Sister  I felt sad and I wanted to hold you.

Mother's Brother  I felt very sad not knowing whether you knew where and when exactly I died, but very glad that I could come back and see you and for you to see me.

Hellinger  How does the father feel?

Father  I felt very full of love for my daughter and gratitude that she was able to meet my parents, my brothers and sisters, and that I could introduce her to them properly for the first time. It meant a lot to me.

Hellinger  And mother?

Mother  I felt, most especially in these last few minutes, the light in my daughter and my heart has been aching to embrace that light because I lost so many people and I thought, she is alive, this one.

Hellinger  Her brother?

Deceased Brother  At first I felt very detached, and then I felt acknowledged and needed, and then I felt very brotherly and protective.

Hellinger  All the best to you and peace. Thank you all.


## Remembering

Hellinger *(after a long silence)* to group: In Germany, we are often told that we must not forget – we must remember what has happened.

It's often said in an accusing and superior way. That has a bad effect in the soul. The appropriate way of remembering is what we have experienced here: grieving for and with the dead. This way of remembering is humble and has a healing and reconciling effect.

# Esther*

## Her father's father committed suicide, his mother and sisters were murdered in a concentration camp

### Summary

The entanglements: *Esther's father was Jewish. When he was still a child, his father committed suicide. His sister, his mother, and many of his mother's sisters were murdered in a concentration camp. Her father was a political prisoner for many years. Esther is an invalid and her sister has attempted suicide many times.*

The resolution: *Esther and her father stand before the dead. The father takes his daughters by the hand and bows deeply before his father, saying, "Dear Papa, I've missed you. These are my children. Look, life has continued on. Please, bless me and my family." Then, he embraces his father and his children. Esther says to her grandfather, "Dear Grandpa, I take you as my grandfather. Bless me as your granddaughter. Now I give you a place in my heart."*

*Then the father, with his daughters, bows down to his mother. Esther tells her, "Dear Grandma, after a while, I'll come, too. In honour of you, I'll stay a while longer."*

*Then Esther's father bows down to his dead sister. Esther says to her, "Dear Aunt, I'll stay on a while, then I'll come, too. Look kindly on me when I stay on a while."*

*Then the father stands next to his wife in view of his dead family and the daughters stand next to their mother. The father tells his wife, "I take you now as my wife." He tells the dead, "This is my wife and these are my children. Please, look kindly on us. You have a place in our hearts. And we'll come, too."*

* Course in Graz, Austria

HELLINGER *to group* This woman is from Croatia, and is accompanied by her therapist. It may be that we'll have to have some translation, so I ask for your patience with this process.

*To Esther* What is this about?

ESTHER I had an operation on my spine 20 years ago, and have been an invalid ever since. At the moment I'm interested in looking at my own self-destructiveness, because I have a feeling that my medical condition is connected to that. There has been a lot of self-destructive behaviour in my family as well as a lot of violence from external sources. I can say that I'm less self-destructive now than I was. There is one thing I always say that's very important and that is, that I can withstand anything. This sentence has been good for me, but it's also sometimes bad.

HELLINGER First, I want to explain something. Any interpretation a person makes that belittles themselves is false, as when someone says that they have self-aggressive tendencies. That's been my experience.

ESTHER What does that mean?

HELLINGER It means that to make progress, you have to give up a negative interpretation. Is that difficult for you?

ESTHER Yes. *(Laughs)*

HELLINGER Exactly. That's the first healing step, that you give up a negative interpretation. No one deserves that. I don't deserve it, and no one else deserves my negative interpretations. What moves us deeply in our souls is positive.

ESTHER I also believe that I can make positive steps. It's not just a belief, I know it.

HELLINGER What moves us deeply in our souls is love. Often, however, you don't know where you stand. You have to find out where you love. And that's what we're going to do. So, you have a father, a mother, and how many brothers and sisters?

ESTHER My mother is dead. I've got my father and one sister.

HELLINGER When did your mother die?

ESTHER Three and a half years ago.

HELLINGER Was either of your parents in another significant relationship?

ESTHER No.

HELLINGER What special events have happened in your family?

ESTHER My father is Jewish and his family were murdered in a concentration camp. When my father was just a boy, his father committed suicide. That's a family secret, but as happens with family secrets, I know it.

HELLINGER  Everyone knows it. So, once more, your father is Jewish and his family were murdered in a concentration camp. Who exactly was killed?

ESTHER  His mother and many aunts – I didn't know any of them. He had a sister who was supposedly pregnant when she was killed.

HELLINGER  His mother was killed and his sister. Were there any other brothers or sisters who were killed?

ESTHER  On his mother's side, yes.

HELLINGER  And did your father's father kill himself in connection with this pogrom?

ESTHER  No, that was before World War II.

HELLINGER  And on your mother's side? What's happened there?

ESTHER  On my mother's side, there's not much. But I've got a sister who has attempted suicide many times.

HELLINGER  How did your accident happen?

ESTHER  I didn't have an accident, it was an inflammation. I was in a lot of pain and I had an operation. Since then I've been an invalid.

HELLINGER  As a result of the operation?

ESTHER  Yes, that's the result.

HELLINGER  Do you suffer gladly or with difficulty?

ESTHER  I suffer gladly.

HELLINGER  Do you know what that means?

ESTHER  Yes, inside me I know what it means. I understand what you mean.

HELLINGER  It means: I love. That's what it means.

ESTHER  Yes.

HELLINGER  Close your eyes and breathe deeply. Allow room for the love.

*Esther closes her eyes and breathes heavily.*

HELLINGER *(after a while)*  I've got another question. How did your father survive?

ESTHER  With difficulty. During the war he was also in prison with the partisans and afterwards he was a political prisoner for six years in a notorious prison. From when I was three until I was nine, my father was in prison and we were alone with my mother. It was a very precarious situation. My mother was also in prison for a year, just because she was his wife.

HELLINGER  Are you married?

ESTHER  No, I live alone.

HELLINGER  Have you got any children?

ESTHER  No.

HELLINGER  Okay, let's set up the constellation. We need representatives for your father, your mother, your sister, and you. We'll start with those.

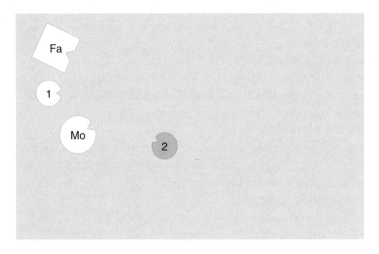

| | |
|---|---|
| Fa | Father |
| Mo | Mother |
| 1 | First child, a daughter |
| **2** | **Second child, a daughter (Esther)** |

HELLINGER  How is the father doing?

FATHER  My legs are shaking. I'm looking straight ahead. I'm experiencing relatively little contact, and a really strange trembling in my legs.

HELLINGER  And the mother?

MOTHER  I haven't got any relationships, and I barely dare to look forward, although I want to. I feel a heavy weight from the right, from my youngest daughter.

HELLINGER  How's the elder sister?

FIRST CHILD  Isolated and I'm being pulled out.

HELLINGER  *to Esther's representative*  And you?

ESTHER'S REPRESENTATIVE It's difficult. On the one hand, I look at my family, on the other hand, I've got nothing to do with them. I feel like they're there, and I'm looking at them, but otherwise there's nothing.

HELLINGER *to Esther* I'm wondering what happened in your mother's family – for example, with her parents or their brothers and sisters.

ESTHER My mother had a good relationship with her father, but not with her mother. She didn't love her mother. I didn't know my grandparents, but my mother was very hurt by her mother.

HELLINGER That's not important. Did someone die?

ESTHER My mother's parents died young.

HELLINGER What's young?

ESTHER For me, young is before I was born. They were about 65 or so.

HELLINGER Well, the father wants to leave, and the mother wants to leave as well. They both want out. Why, I don't know.

*Hellinger moves the mother further away.*

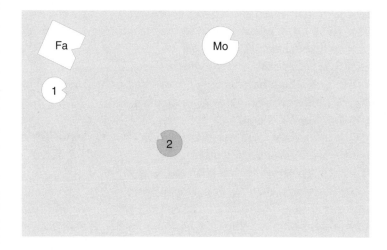

HELLINGER How's that?

MOTHER It's no good. I have to have something to do with what's behind me.

*Hellinger returns the mother to her place and adds a representative for the father's father, who killed himself, and the father's mother and sister, who were killed in a concentration camp.*

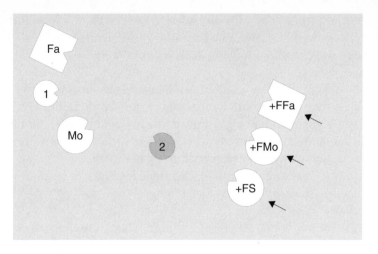

FFA   Father's father, who committed suicide when the father was a child
FMo   Father's mother, who was murdered in a concentration camp
FS    Father's sister, who was murdered in a concentration camp

HELLINGER  What has changed?

FATHER  There's a lot of energy and shivery feelings and … *(he breathes out several times, aloud).*

HELLINGER *to elder sister*  And for you?

FIRST CHILD  Nothing has changed for me. But, before, a lot changed when my mother was standing there in front of me.

HELLINGER  What was that?

FIRST CHILD  I had the feeling then that I didn't have to leave. The pull from out there was suddenly gone.

HELLINGER *to mother*  What has changed for you?

MOTHER  Shivering, shaking. A powerful change.

HELLINGER *to Esther's representative*  And for you?

ESTHER'S REPRESENTATIVE  When my mother was standing over there, I felt better for a little while. Now, I feel a lot of strength from behind me. When my mother was further away, it was better, but even where she is it's not as bad, because of them back there.

HELLINGER *to Esther*  Something must have happened in your mother's family. Do you know what was said?

ESTHER  Yes. My mother wasn't accepted by her mother-in-law because my father's mother wanted him to marry a Jewish woman. So they never had any relationship with each other.

150

HELLINGER That's not important here.

*Hellinger moves Esther's representative so that she can see the representatives of the dead.*

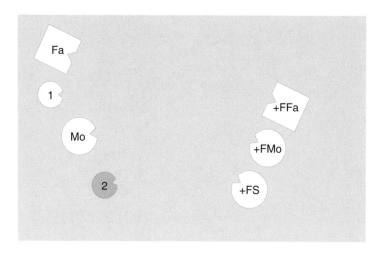

HELLINGER *to father's father* How are you feeling?
FATHER'S FATHER I'm fine. My wife is next to me, which is good, and I like looking at my son.
FATHER'S MOTHER I'm swaying a bit.
FATHER'S SISTER I've got a pain in my neck.

*Hellinger places the father with the dead.*

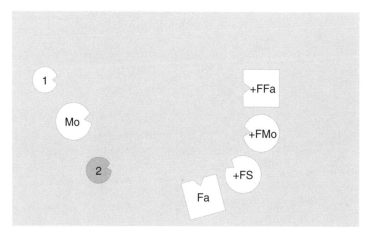

HELLINGER *to father* How's that?
FATHER That's better.
HELLINGER *to Esther's representative* And for you?
ESTHER'S REPRESENTATIVE I feel very unimportant.
HELLINGER Go and stand next to him.

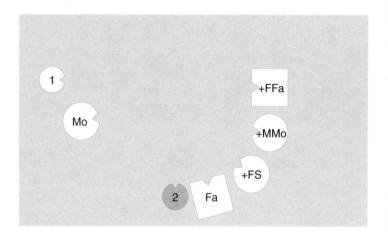

HELLINGER How's that?
ESTHER'S REPRESENTATIVE I'm afraid, but I'm feeling better.
FATHER I'm shaking a bit more again. I've got more energy.

*Hellinger asks the father to take his two daughters by the hand and to stand in front of his father and bow down before him with his daughters.*

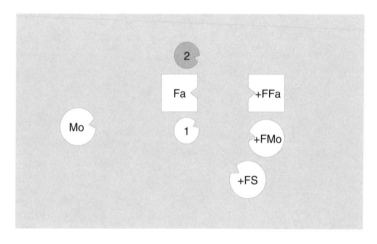

HELLINGER *to father*  Now stand up straight and say, "Dear Papa."
FATHER  Dear papa.
HELLINGER  "I've missed you."
FATHER  I've missed you.
HELLINGER  How is that for his father?
FATHER'S FATHER  I feel touched. It's lovely.
HELLINGER *to father*  Tell him, "These are my children."
FATHER  These are my children.
HELLINGER  "Look, life has continued on."
FATHER  Look, life has continued on.
HELLINGER  "Please bless me and my family."
FATHER  Please bless me and my family.
HELLINGER  Go to him with your children and all of you put your arms around him.
*To Esther (after a while, as they finish their embrace)*  Will you take your place with them?
　*To father*  Take her by the hand and go to her grandfather again with her.


*Esther embraces her grandfather, sobbing.*


HELLINGER  Breathe deeply, in and out. Just so, yes.
*After a while*  Say to him, "Dear Grandpa." Say it in your mother tongue.
ESTHER *(in Croatian)*  Dear Grandpa.
HELLINGER  "I take you as my grandfather."
ESTHER  I take you as my grandfather.
HELLINGER  "And bless me as your granddaughter."
ESTHER  And bless me as your granddaughter.
HELLINGER  "Now I give you a place in my heart."
ESTHER  Now I give you a place in my heart.
HELLINGER  Breathe deeply. Just like that.
*After a while*  Now, take a step back.
*To father*  Take her by the hand now and go to her grandmother.


*Meanwhile, the grandfather has spontaneously moved behind the grandmother.*

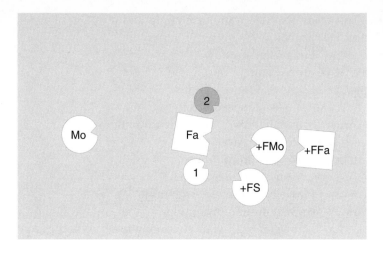

HELLINGER *to Esther*  Say, "Dear Grandma."
ESTHER  Dear Grandma.
HELLINGER *(as he sees that Esther is very moved)*  Go to her.

*Esther stands in front of her grandmother, looks at her for a long time, then embraces her warmly. Esther's father also moves to his mother and embraces her together with Esther. The grandfather puts his arm around the grandmother's shoulders. Esther sobs aloud.*

HELLINGER *(after a while) to Esther*  Open your eyes and look at your grandmother. Remain in your embrace, but look her in the eye. Tell her, "I'll come, too." *Esther sighs deeply.* Look at her! Tell her, "After a while, I'll come, too.
ESTHER  After a while, then I'll come, too. *(She weeps.)*
HELLINGER *(after a pause)*  Now tell her, "In honour of you, I'll stay a while longer."
ESTHER *(laughs)*  In honour of you, I'll stay a while longer. Yes. *(She sighs deeply.)*
HELLINGER  How is the grandmother feeling?
FATHER'S MOTHER  Yes, she should stay.
HELLINGER *to Esther*  Good. Now go to the aunt.

*The father takes his two daughters by the hand and stands with them in front of his dead sister.*

154

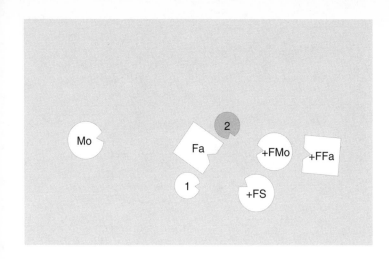

HELLINGER *to Esther* Say, "Dear Aunt."
ESTHER Dear Aunt.
HELLINGER Bow down to her, all three of you. Then, all three of you go to her.

*The three go to the aunt and embrace her.*

HELLINGER *(after a while) to Esther* Look at her and tell her, "I'll stay a while longer."
ESTHER I'll stay a while longer.
HELLINGER Look kindly when I stay on a while.
ESTHER Look kindly when I stay on a while.
FATHER'S SISTER Happily.

*Hellinger places the father next to his wife and the children next to their mother. They form a semi-circle. He moves the dead somewhat closer to the family.*

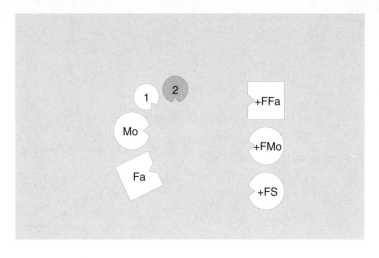

HELLINGER  How's the father doing?

FATHER  Good.

HELLINGER  The mother?

MOTHER  Finally, solid ground.

FIRST CHILD  Relieved.

ESTHER  Loving.

HELLINGER  Exactly. That's it. Can you see the difference?
*To father* Tell your wife, "I take you now as my wife."

FATHER  I take you now as my wife.

HELLINGER  Tell your dead family, "This is my wife."

FATHER  This is my wife.

HELLINGER  "And these are my children."

FATHER  And these are my children.

HELLINGER  "Look kindly on us."

FATHER  Please, look kindly on us.

HELLINGER  "You have a place in our hearts."

FATHER  You have a place in our hearts.

HELLINGER  "And we'll come, too."

FATHER  And we'll come, too.

HELLINGER  How's the father?

FATHER  Good.

MOTHER  Very good.

FIRST CHILD  Good.

ESTHER  Me, too.

FATHER'S FATHER  Very good.

156

FATHER'S MOTHER  Good.
FATHER'S SISTER  Good.
HELLINGER  Okay, that's it.


## BLESSINGS

HELLINGER *to group*  There are peculiar things that occur repeatedly in such constellations, that we can see and feel. The dead who have departed in such a way feel stifled and they make the living fearful. That was clearly the case here with the mother, who felt a very strong urge to look away. The dead need something, so to speak, in order to find their own peace. That means that the living need to go to them, bow down to them, and honour them. They need to show their love and affirm that life has gone on. Then the dead have their peace and the living have theirs as well. Then, the dead, who have made the living fearful, can be a blessing for them instead. That's what was important here – what was due.

*To Esther*  What do you owe the dead? You owe them something, that's clear. That you're okay – that's what you owe them now.

ESTHER *(laughs)*  Yes, I see that.

HELLINGER  You owe it to the dead for things to be better for you. Agreed? *(Esther nods.)* Good.


## MOURNING

HELLINGER *to group*  There's something very special about Jewish destinies. They have a particular depth and strength and they deserve a deep respect. These destinies deserve a very deep respect. With such a deep respect, we participate with them, but in a healing way. Many people, particularly in Germany and Austria, feel guilty when they come in contact with the fates of Jewish people. Such a guilty feeling is cheap. It accomplishes nothing but discontent and dis-ease on all sides. It brings discontent to the Jewish people as well. But, deep respect in the face of such a destiny, and a grieving together has a healing effect for all.

# Irma*

## Her parents were high-ranking Nazis in Austria

### SUMMARY

The entanglements: *Irma is worried about going insane and having to die, which are feelings taken over from her mother's mother. Both of her mother's parents were high ranking Nazis in Austria. Irma's mother is drawn out of the family. Her father was supposed to have become a priest. His mother released him from that commitment on her deathbed.*

The resolution: *The grandparents are set off to the side, where the grandmother experiences the same anxieties as Irma described earlier. Both grandparents feel better standing off to the side. Irma's mother stands next to her husband. The mother tells her parents, "I'm going to my husband. You have to go."*

*Irma bows down before her father and says, "Daddy, you are my protector." She embraces him and then leans back against him.*

HELLINGER *to Irma* Tell me briefly what the problem is.
IRMA I suffer from anxiety attacks and panic attacks, to the point that I'm afraid I'll go crazy, that I'll become mentally ill. I always think I'm going to die, I have the feeling that I must die.
HELLINGER That's enough.
*To group* She gave me more information earlier, so I can begin immediately now with the work.
*To Irma* We'll set up your father, your mother, and the four children. Was either of your parents in another significant relationship?
IRMA No.
HELLINGER Okay, set up the representatives.

---

* Course in Graz, Austria

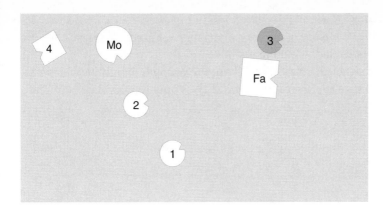

| Fa | Father | 2 | Second child, a daughter |
|----|--------|---|--------------------------|
| Mo | Mother | **3** | **Third child, a daughter (Irma)** |
| 1 | First child, a daughter | 4 | Fourth child, a son |

HELLINGER *to mother* How are you feeling?
MOTHER I'm concerned about two things: "Who is that in front of me?" and, "They are suffering." When the woman in orange came by *(Irma's representative)* – I don't know what she is to me, I mean I only know it intellectually – there was such pain that I was shaking. That's all.

*Hellinger moves her off to the side.*

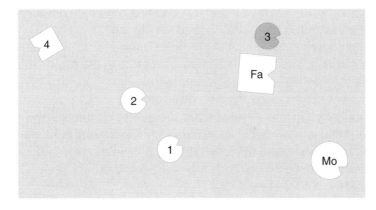

HELLINGER And now?
MOTHER That's better – not completely, but it's better.
HELLINGER How is the father now?

FATHER  At first I felt cut off. I didn't have any idea what I was doing here. When my daughter came, I then realized, all of a sudden, that I was married. Now I feel relieved.

HELLINGER  Turn around. I'll put the younger daughter over here a bit and turn the son around, too. This is only temporary.

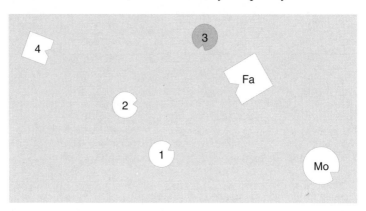

HELLINGER *to father*  How is that now?

FATHER  I feel joyful and also close to tears.

FIRST CHILD  My heart's fluttering and my thighs are quaking. As my mother went by, my vision suddenly sharpened. Before, everything was fuzzy and I didn't want to go anywhere. I looked over there and was totally uninterested.

SECOND CHILD  When my mother was standing behind me, I was completely lame on my left side. She was very threatening. I had a bit of feeling for my elder sister, but she never looked over. When my father turned around, I felt happy at first and then tears came to my eyes.

HELLINGER *to Irma's representative*  And you?

IRMA'S REPRESENTATIVE  Over there in that position I didn't know exactly if that was my father or my brother, I was looking at strangers. Now I see my sisters and brother there and there's a space in front of me that I didn't have before. It was really constricting.

HELLINGER  And the brother?

FOURTH CHILD  Being turned away was very sad. I felt cut off. Now that I've heard my father's voice, I feel a strong connection to him.

*Hellinger arranges the children in order of age opposite the father.*

160

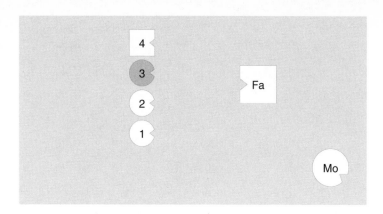

HELLINGER How is it now?

FIRST CHILD It was better immediately as far as the heart flutter and the shaking legs were concerned.

SECOND CHILD Good.

IRMA'S REPRESENTATIVE I can breathe out. Over there my heart was pounding too.

FOURTH CHILD It's fine for me, too.

HELLINGER *to father* And you?

FATHER I'm surprised that I've got such a large family. I feel happy.

HELLINGER *to mother* How are you?

MOTHER As I stood here and heard them behind me, a feeling of heartache came over me rather quickly. Now the tears are coming. I belong there.

HELLINGER Can you hold out a bit longer here? I'll rescue you in a bit.

MOTHER Yes.

HELLINGER *to Irma* How many of your father's sisters and brothers died young?

IRMA Four died young, the first three and the last son. Then my grandfather remarried.

HELLINGER Did your father's mother die in connection with that child?

IRMA She had uterine cancer and the doctors said it could have come from having so many miscarriages and so many children.

*Hellinger adds representatives for the father's parents and his dead siblings and places them next to the father.*

161

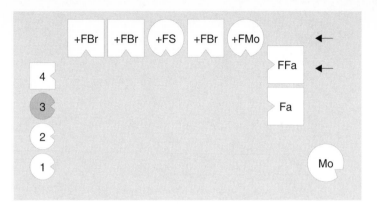

| | |
|---|---|
| FFa | Father's father |
| FMo | Father's mother, who died of uterine cancer |
| FBr | Father's brothers, who died young |
| FS | Fathers sister, who died young |

HELLINGER  How is that?

FATHER  A big relief.

HELLINGER *to father's father*  Tell him, "I'll decide what becomes of you."

FATHER'S FATHER  I'll decide what becomes of you.

HELLINGER *to father*  How does that feel? Just from feeling?

FATHER  Very dominated.

HELLINGER  Is it better or worse?

FATHER  It's clear. I can adapt to that.

HELLINGER  Yes, exactly.

*To Irma*  How is that for you when your grandfather says that to your father?

IRMA  It's his father. It fits.

HELLINGER *to group*  I'll tell you the background information. Irma's father was supposed to become a priest. When he was 13, his mother released him from that promise on her deathbed. She had no right to do that. His father had the responsibility for that decision. That was the background.

*To father*  How are you feeling, now?

FATHER  Now it's even clearer.

HELLINGER  How's the father's mother feeling?

FATHER'S MOTHER  It's fine here.

HELLINGER  And the mother?

MOTHER  Something has moved in my back. I'm not so cut in half. But I want to participate.

162

*Hellinger moves her next to her husband.*

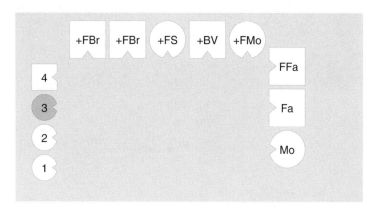

MOTHER  I know who they are. *(Laughing, she indicates the children.)*
HELLINGER  How is that for the husband, now that she's next to you?
FATHER  Completely new. I hadn't reckoned with her.
*(Laughter in room)*
HELLINGER  Once destined for the priesthood, always destined for the priesthood. Says another authority besides your father.
*To Irma's representative*  How are you doing now?
IRMA'S REPRESENTATIVE  I don't know. I don't have any clear feelings. I smiled just now at what happened. It's all still somewhat unclear. I have to remind myself that she's my mother. She seems more alive now. It's like she was moved to that place by remote control.
HELLINGER *to Irma*  What happened with your mother's parents?
IRMA  They were important Nazis.
HELLINGER  Both of them?
IRMA  Yes.
HELLINGER  Set up representatives for them.

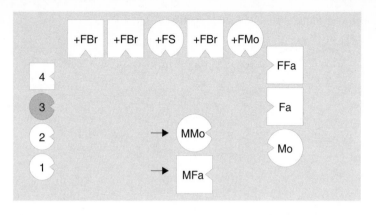

MFa    Mother's father
MMo    Mothers' mother

HELLINGER *to grandmother* How is it?
GRANDMOTHER It seems like a tribunal here, that's going to judge me. *(She breathes heavily.)*
HELLINGER *to Irma* Who is afraid?
IRMA My grandmother?
HELLINGER Who's afraid of going insane?
IRMA My grandmother?
HELLINGER Who's afraid of having to die?
IRMA My grandmother?
HELLINGER Exactly. Take your place.
*To Irma's brother and sisters who are also present:* And all of you take your places in the constellation. That's good for everyone. You can hold hands.

*Irma and her brother and sisters take their places in the constellation.*

HELLINGER *to mother* How are you now?
MOTHER When my parents came in I started hurting on the left side again, and I thought, "Get away. You're blocking my view of my children." I feel connected to my husband. And now, I could cry.
HELLINGER *to father* How's this for you?
FATHER It's like a threat and a disruption. I'm happy about my children.
HELLINGER *to mother* Tell your parents, "I'm going to my husband."

164

MOTHER  I'm going to my husband.
HELLINGER  *"You* have to go."
MOTHER  *You* have to get out of the way.
HELLINGER  No, only, *"You* have to go."
MOTHER  *You* have to go.
HELLINGER  *to mother's father*  How's that for you?
MOTHER'S FATHER  It's okay. I'm in this together with my wife.
GRANDMOTHER  Exactly. It's good like this.
HELLINGER  Go over there and turn around.

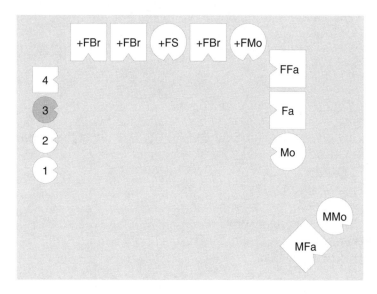

HELLINGER  How is that now?
MOTHER'S FATHER  It's fine like this.
GRANDMOTHER  Fine.
HELLINGER  *to Irma*  How are you feeling?
IRMA  Now that they're gone, I feel fine. *(Crying)* I'd like to go over
there to my parents.
HELLINGER  Yes, that's exactly what you have to do. Now we've got to
chase out the bad spirits. Go to your father, follow your impulse.

*Irma stands in front of her father and bows down to him.*

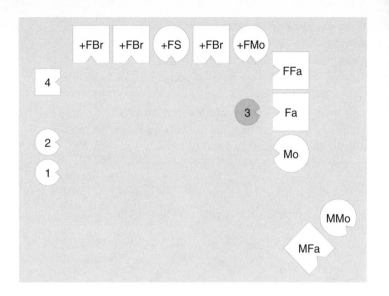

HELLINGER *(after a while)* Straighten up again. How did you address your father?
IRMA Daddy.
HELLINGER say, "Daddy."
IRMA Daddy.
HELLINGER "You're my protector."
IRMA You're my protector. *(She cries.)*
HELLINGER Go to him.

*Irma goes to her father and embraces him, sobbing.*

HELLINGER *to group* What's so macabre is that the husband had to live with these in-laws. He became very depressive. No wonder! He absorbed it all and it was Hell. I can say out-and-out that no one could remain normal in such a situation.
*To mother* You have to go to your husband, not the other way around. That's the resolution here. Can you feel it?
MOTHER I'm so happy that he's there for the children.
HELLINGER Yes, that he is, now.
*To the other children* How are you doing now?
FIRST CHILD It's much better now that the grandparents are out.
SECOND CHILD It feels good that my mother is really standing by my father.

166

HELLINGER *to Irma (as she finishes embracing her father)* How are you feeling now?
IRMA Good.
HELLINGER Now lean back against your father.

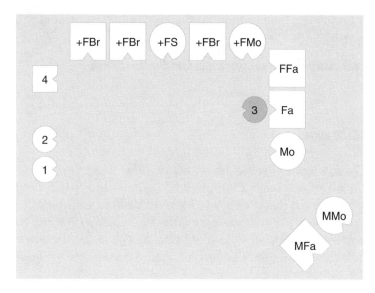

IRMA *(after a while)* He's a good father.
HELLINGER I think so, too. Okay, that's it.

## Samuel*

### His parents and brother were murdered in Auschwitz

#### Background

##### Excerpts from a letter from Samuel, July 20, 1996

My good friend, Juana Danis, psychotherapist and founder of the Institute for Psycho-symbolism, Munich, sent me your book, *"Anerkennen, was ist"* (*Acknowledging What Is*). I couldn't put the book down. Your work, your style of working, and above all, the way you handle the family constellations, all made a deep impression on me and I was moved to tears.

My parents were Viennese, and I was born on 14 July 1920 in Prague. My mother tongue was German, our 'mother's helper' spoke Czech, and I attended a Slovakian primary school, a German 'Real-gymnasium' and then finished my 'Matura' in a Slovakian school. In addition, I had private instruction in French, English, written Hebrew, and even Gabelsberger shorthand. My father was a stenographer in the court of the Austro-Hungarian Monarchy at the turn of the century.

Although it seems like yesterday, it's been 58 years and ten days since I left our home in Pressburg to go to Lyon to study chemistry. At the time of the events in Munich, I was living in Paris, where I requested an American immigration visa. I was granted the visa in March 1943 in Cuba. My mother and my brother, Heinz Georg (born in 1927) were murdered in Auschwitz in March 1942. My 63 year old father met the same fate in July.

As a chemist in the defence industry, I was not in a situation to be able to fight in the war, but as an American soldier, I was able to join

---

* Course in London (2)

168

a group of German-speaking engineers, who achieved some positive things. After the war I was able to even things up some. I built a successful chemical concern that then expanded into Europe, South America, and much of the rest of the world and I've made a considerable contribution to the development of Israel. Last but not at all least, I have a family once again.

But … as an acquaintance said to me recently, "We all still live in Dachau." Life in exile is difficult, and more so when 'home' no longer exists. The 'survivors' syndrome' of concentration camp survivors, first described by my therapist, Dr. Niederland, resists successful treatment. I could see this in my cousin Franzi, who survived Dr. Mengele and Auschwitz. Her first child, Helen Epstein, is the author of *"Children of the Holocaust"* in which she describes how the syndrome can also be seen in the children of survivors. A psychiatrist in Israel has described symptoms passed on to the third and fourth generations!

My guardian angel kept me from the hands of the Nazis, and my 'survivors' syndrome' was never as severe as Franzi's, but I had to – had to! – try to make some contribution, however small, to bring about a healing of this horror.

In 1973, I discovered Therese Bertherat's *"Le Corps a Ses Raisons."* The book deals with an approach to psychotherapy through physiotherapy, in that the muscles mirror the psyche. If one can make the muscles and movement healthier, more symmetrical, and more harmonious, then the movements of the spirit – feelings – also become healthier, more symmetrical and harmonious.

A student of Bertherat, Dr. Eileen Miles, was in New York, and treated Franzi Epstein. She didn't achieve much, as Franzi's experiences in the camp had weakened her so much that she was unable to do much physically. I learned a lot from Dr. Miles, however, and at her recommendation I turned to Professor Gendlin (Focusing).

Dr Niederland was of the old school. After twelve years of working with him, I asked him (twenty years ago) what could be achieved through analysis. His answer was, "According to Sigmund Freud, "At best, a certain discontent"."

"But you know I only want one thing – I want to go home!" I said. "I know it's no longer there, it's impossible, and could never be possible. I'm a child of a world that was gone when I was born. I want to go back to pre-war Vienna."

"We can't help you with that," he replied.

Then your book arrived, offering just such a return. Could you, would you, help me to set up my family constellation? Would you accept me as a patient? Is 76 too old? I ask you for a ten minute appointment by telephone.

P.S. I have scarcely written German in the last 50 years, since 1943. I have just read this letter over and must immodestly say that it's rather well written. I probably could have written it in English in an hour's less time. The thoughts, dictated by my father, brought bitter tears and the awareness that your book has already given me something of value.

### Excerpt from the letter of reply, August 3, 1996

Your letter has touched me deeply and I will try to accommodate your wishes as far as I am able. Since I am, myself, 70 years old, I offer very few courses. I normally work with a small circle of patients or clients, setting up family constellations in front of a large audience of therapists. I would be happy to have you set up your family constellation in such a setting. The next possible opportunity would be a course in London which is being offered 24–26 January 1997.

There are also some possibilities in Germany and I enclose an information flyer. If you wish to participate in one of these courses, please let me know. I will make sure that you get a place on a course.

If you wish to work on this theme more thoroughly, I recommend a course with my friend, Dr. Hunter Beaumont. He is an American living in Munich. He is very familiar with the work, particularly the work with Holocaust survivors. He offers courses in London for smaller groups, where there is more time available for each individual.

I am very grateful to you.
Yours,
*Bert Hellinger*

## SUMMARY

The fate: *Both Samuel's parents and his brother were murdered in Auschwitz. He was saved with the help of his mother's brother. His paternal grandmother committed suicide at the grave of her illegitimate son, who had died of appendicitis. His maternal grandmother committed suicide following the death of her husband.*

The resolution: *Samuel stands with his murdered parents and his murdered brother. He says to them, "This is my place. Here, I belong." Everyone feels very moved. As Samuel tells them, "I have two children. Life continues on." the faces of the dead family members light up. Samuel says to them, "In a little while, I will join you. I will come too."*

HELLINGER  Now I'll work with you and I won't say anything about your background, I'll just let you set up your family of origin. Who belongs to it: your father, your mother, ... who else? How many children?

SAMUEL  I have a brother, an uncle, and somebody you brought out in me. Heinrich, my father's brother, who died of an undiagnosed appendicitis at a time when he was the only support of his family, and my grandmother, my father's mother, Heinrich's mother, who many, many years later, committed suicide on his grave. And perhaps one more, an aunt of my father's. She owned a bar and was a Talmud scholar in the 1880's-1890's, which was a completely unheard of thing.

HELLINGER  How many brothers and sisters do you have?

SAMUEL  One brother.

HELLINGER  Who's older, you or him?

SAMUEL  He's younger. He was murdered in Auschwitz.

HELLINGER  I'll start with your father, your mother, your brother, and you.

*Samuel chooses and sets up representatives.*

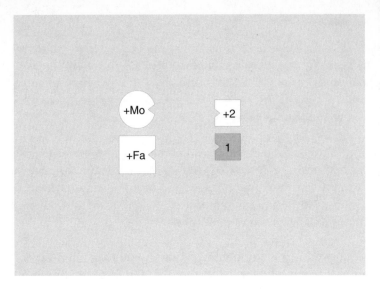

Fa   Father
Mo   Mother
**1    First child, a son (Samuel)**
2    Second child, a son, who was murdered in Auschwitz

HELLINGER *(noticing that the father's representative is staring down at the floor) to Samuel* What happened in your father's family?

SAMUEL His father, my father's father, died rather young. There were three children. My father had a sister and a brother. I'm sorry, two brothers. They were in Vienna. The oldest brother, Heinrich, died of appendicitis. I repeat myself.

HELLINGER That's okay, do that. We need that.

SAMUEL My grandmother eventually committed suicide. This Heinrich may have been an illegitimate child. May have been, I have no idea. I was told that by my aunt's daughter, Franzi. Perhaps it's a rumour. But yesterday and today, this Heinrich became Uncle Heinrich.

HELLINGER Choose somebody for this Uncle Heinrich and your grandmother and set them up too. *(He does so.)*

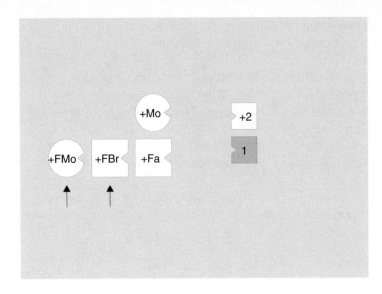

FMo   Father's mother, who committed suicide
FBr   Father's brother, who died of appendicitis

HELLINGER *to father (who is still staring at the floor)* Now, what's going on?

FATHER I'm feeling very heavy and sad and isolated. I don't connect.

HELLINGER *to father's brother* I think I must put you here *(moves uncle and grandmother)*.

*As his brother stands next to him, the father slowly straightens up.*

HELLINGER *to father* Just turn towards him.

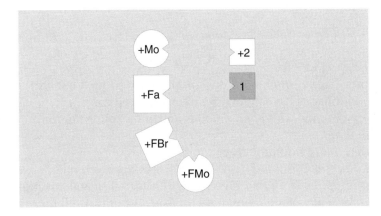

173

The father embraces his brother warmly. Then they move apart and look into each other's eyes for a long time.

FATHER I'm seeing his loving eyes. That's what I needed.
HELLINGER *to father's brother* What was going on with you?
FATHER'S BROTHER I felt a deep weakness behind him, and now a very good feeling seeing him.
HELLINGER Now, the grandmother?
PATERNAL GRANDMOTHER I can't bear watching it.

*Hellinger adds another male to represent the father of the father's illegitimate brother and one for the father's father. He moves the children further back.*

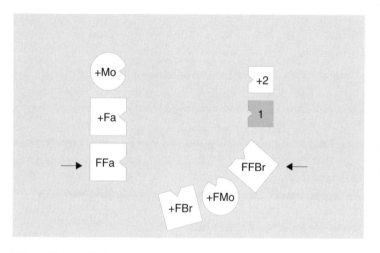

FFa    Father's father
FFBr   Father of the father's half-brother

*To father* How's that?
FATHER That's better, but I don't feel connected with my wife. It's extraordinary, I haven't seen her or experienced her.
HELLINGER Wait. This is your mother and this is your wife. You meant your wife?
FATHER Yes, I meant my wife.
HELLINGER *to father's brother* What's going on with you now?
FATHER'S BROTHER I had a quite strange feeling when my father came in … kind of wobbly knees. It seems to get better now, I think.

HELLINGER His mother?

PATERNAL GRANDMOTHER Blank.

PATERNAL GRANDMOTHER'S FORMER PARTNER I feel calm, as if I should be here.

HELLINGER *to Samuel's representative* What's going on with you?

SAMUEL'S REPRESENTATIVE It's better now that I've moved back. I can look at my brother. I had two intense lines of pain in my chest and they've lessened. The feeling of responsibility was overwhelming and I don't want to look at that, I want to escape.

*Hellinger has the brothers change places.*

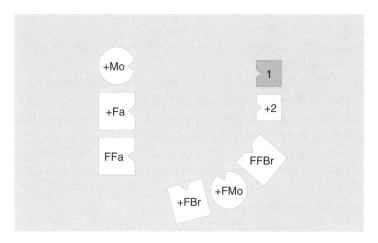

SAMUEL'S REPRESENTATIVE For the first time I see my mother.

HELLINGER *to Samuel* That's the right order. You must take the first place and he takes second place. It always goes clockwise.

*To Samuel's brother* You?

CHILD 2 Here I've started shivering. My father's seeing me for the first time. Now my brother feels more like my big brother. I was very fearful for all the family and especially my brother before. Very fearful. This feels much better

HELLINGER The mother? The wife?

MOTHER I feel very hot. I'm burning up on this side. I thought I had a fever. This is better but I still … my hand is wet and hot.

HELLINGER *to Samuel* What happened in the family of your mother?

SAMUEL I must first say that my father ran away and went into the navy and did all sorts of other things. He freed himself for a time.

What happened in the family of my mother? I was told that my grandmother committed suicide after the death of my grandfather. I did not know that as a child. I heard that many years later, and again as a rumour. The two brothers, who were both successful entrepreneurs, fought and separated. I was beholden to both of them. They saved my life. I'm angry at one of them because he didn't, they didn't save my parents, which they could have. I've never said that out loud.

HELLINGER  What happened to your parents?

SAMUEL  They were deported in '42 from Bratislava-Pressburg and murdered in Auschwitz.

HELLINGER  Both your parents?

SAMUEL  Both my parents and my brother.

HELLINGER  The father of your mother, what did he die of? Your maternal grandfather?

SAMUEL  My maternal grandfather, died of a heart problem.

HELLINGER  Who was the one who saved you?

SAMUEL  My mother's brothers, my uncles, were the ones who helped me to get out of France where I was going to school.

HELLINGER  Just to get quite it clear, who were the people who were murdered in the Nazi concentration camps? Your father, your mother …

SAMUEL  And my brother.

HELLINGER  Any other members of your family?

SAMUEL  Not of my immediate family. Many others further removed.

HELLINGER  Who?

SAMUEL  My family in Prague, with a few exceptions. I did not know them too well. I must turn it around. Many survived, and survived well. My cousin Franzi survived Auschwitz. Her daughter wrote "Children of the Holocaust" and started a whole movement. Many of my friends … I was a member of a swim club … almost a champion … many of them survived … a third of them survived, two thirds of them survived.

HELLINGER *to mother*  What's going on?

MOTHER  I'm just burning up on the right hand side. This whole side of my body is so hot. This side is cooler. It's extremely uncomfortable.

HELLINGER  I think I'll bring in your mother.

176

*Hellinger selects a representative for the mother's mother, who killed her-self, and places her behind the mother.*

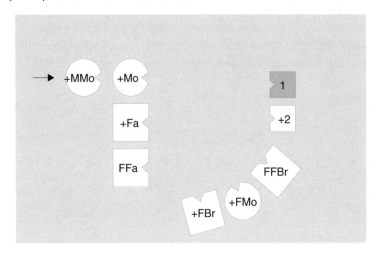

MMo   Mother's mother, who killed herself

HELLINGER  Is that better?
MOTHER  It's better, but I'm still very warm on this side of my body. But it's more balanced.

*Hellinger moves the murdered brother [child 2] between his parents.*

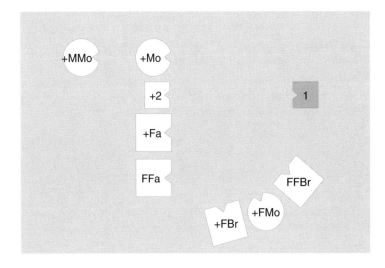

HELLINGER  How's that?

MOTHER  It's an enormous relief.

CHILD 2  I've had the same feverish symptoms that my mother's described and I'm still very hot. I feel better here. I'm all sweaty.

FATHER  That was an enormous relief to me. I don't know this woman. My wife? I don't understand how I could have married her.

*Hellinger rearranges representatives.*

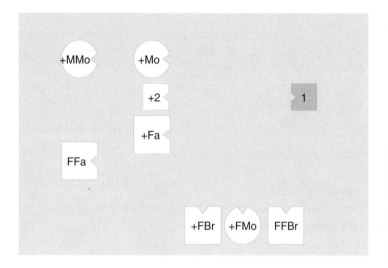

HELLINGER *to Samuel's representative*  How are you feeling now?

SAMUEL'S REPRESENTATIVE  I feel relieved. I feel … I'm starting to sway and my body is not shaking anymore. I'm very confused and I don't understand anything, but I feel relief.

*Hellinger brings Samuel himself into the constellation. He places him opposite his parents and brother, looking at them.*

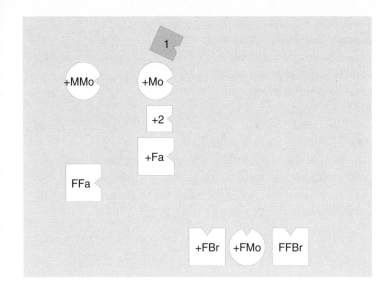

HELLINGER *to Samuel* Just stand at the side of your mother, as if you would join them. Look at them with love.

*Samuel is visibly moved.*

HELLINGER *(after a while)* Tell them, "That's my place." Look at them.
SAMUEL This is my place. It is. That's where I am. *He looks at his family and weeps.*
MOTHER *(after a while)* I'm sorry. It feels right and I'm sorry.
HELLINGER *to Samuel* Repeat it. "This is my place."
SAMUEL This is my place.
HELLINGER "Here, I'm at home."
SAMUEL Hier gehöre ich.
HELLINGER That's right, "Here I belong."
SAMUEL Here I belong.
HELLINGER How's the father feeling?
FATHER I give him my blessing.
HELLINGER The brother?
CHILD 2 *(very moved)* I give him my blessing too. I really feel the burden he's carried. It's awful.
MOTHER I feel very sad. But peacefully sad.
HELLINGER *to Samuel* Tell them, "I have children." Have you? How many children do you have?

SAMUEL  Two.

HELLINGER  Tell them, "I have two children."

SAMUEL  I have two children.

HELLINGER  "Life is going on."

SAMUEL  And life is going on.

MOTHER  I'm glad.

CHILD 2  I'm glad, too.

FATHER  That's the greatest happiness for me.

HELLINGER  Tell them, "A little while, then I will come too."

SAMUEL  A little while and I will join you. I will come too.

HELLINGER *to Samuel*  Can I leave it like that? *Samuel nods.*
*To representatives*  Thank you all.

# Elisabeth*
## "You have looked afar"

HELLINGER *to Elisabeth, who has cancer* Are you ready?
ELISABETH Yes.
HELLINGER You've been looking afar.
ELISABETH Afar?
HELLINGER You've been looking into the distance.
ELISABETH That's true.
HELLINGER And how is it there?
ELISABETH Actually, lovely.
HELLINGER Exactly. You've crossed the boundary.
ELISABETH Yes.
HELLINGER There's no fear there.
ELISABETH I don't think there is.
HELLINGER Exactly. The soul isn't afraid of death. The soul is drawn back to its source. At the source, everything is in good keeping. There, nothing and no one gets lost. Many people are afraid that they have to preserve something, nature or something. At the source, nature can't get lost, nor can people, neither the good nor the bad. No one is left out there.

There's a movement in the soul with a yearning to return to the source. When the time is right, the soul leans towards this and is at peace. It's a beautiful movement. When I look at you, it seems you have made this movement. There's an unbelievable beauty in this movement – an unbelievable depth. What is all our talk of health and happiness compared to this deep movement? It's the most profound movement of all.

* Course in Kassel

There are some, though, who make this movement too soon. They intervene in the natural process and damage the soul. They have to be restrained, because to make such a movement before its time is an abuse. The process is actually peacefully calm. I think that's all I may say to you.

*The following day*

## Her father was half Jewish

### SUMMARY

The entanglements: *Elisabeth's mother refused to marry Elisabeth's father because he was half Jewish, even though, as a well known artist he was granted permission to marry from Hitler himself. The mother atones for this in her desire to leave. Instead of her mother leaving, Elisabeth wants to leave with her children. Elisabeth, like her mother, has separated from her husband.*

The resolution: *Elisabeth's children are placed with their father. Her mother says to Elisabeth's father, "I'll go instead of you." Then, she moves off to the side.*

*Elisabeth says to her father, You are the right one." She says to her mother, "I'll go instead of you." It is clear that Elisabeth's mother is drawing her into death. Elisabeth's father, however, tells her, "You stay here." She tells her father, "I have scorned you as my mother did. I've been ashamed of you and have denied you. Now, I'm sorry. Let me come to you." She kneels down before him and bows all the way to the floor. She says, "I'm a Jew, like you." Then she tells her mother, "I'm a Jew, like Papa."*

*Her mother says to Elisabeth's father, "I've done you an injustice and I leave our daughter with you." Elisabeth tells her children "This is my father, a Jew." She says to her husband, "I acknowledge the fact that you married me, even though I'm Jewish." She realizes that she has driven her husband away, just as her mother had driven away her husband, Elisabeth's father, and she tells him, "I exonerate you."*

HELLINGER *to Elisabeth*  What does your soul have to say?
ELISABETH  That I still have something to resolve.
HELLINGER  In your present family or your family of origin?
ELISABETH  Both, really, because I believe they're connected.
HELLINGER  Are you married?

ELISABETH  Yes.

HELLINGER  How many children?

ELISABETH  Two children. My husband left me 12 years ago. It was a very difficult separation. Then, three years ago I got cancer, and indeed, very severely. There have been huge operations and chemotherapy for the last three years. A few times they gave me up for lost, but I've always pulled through. One thing I haven't managed, though, is to let go of my husband. For years I identified with his new wife and their life together and always felt totally shattered – I didn't really exist. After the separation I was severely depressed for years, and always thought about how I could kill myself. I was also chemically dependent. I've made it through that though. Actually, I've found my way back to life through this terrible illness. But, I've wanted to really resolve this the way you described earlier. I've wanted to have a harmonious relationship with my husband and also with my mother, but I always move into a victim role, because that's the only way I can stand firm. I didn't want to lose them. I avoid any guilt of my own, but then I bring others, my husband, for example, into the role of having to feel guilty. So, I can't really let go with feeling, although I know that I want to.

HELLINGER  I want to say something about innocence. Some people dream of being and remaining innocent. In that way, they remain children. Innocents are children who want to remain children. You remain fundamentally limited.

ELISABETH  That way you don't hurt anyone.

HELLINGER  Oh yes you do. The morally superior spread an atmosphere of aggression around them, and one gets nasty with them. That allows the moral ones to feel like victims, too, and they puff up even bigger.

ELISABETH  But that's terrible. There's a lot of aggression there that's just repressed.

HELLINGER  Exactly that. Once, in one of my courses, there was a student of the Maharishi of Transcendental Meditation. Nothing against Transcendental Meditation, far from it. She said that it was wonderful that when meditating, you can be completely detached. I asked her what happened then around her. She said her husband always got very aggressive. That's not the fault of Transcendental Meditation, but because of the belief that you can remove yourself and disconnect. That causes others to get angry. Those who think they are better are always persecuted. Very peculiar.

ELISABETH  I've always set myself apart.

HELLINGER  We'll set up your present family: your husband, yourself, and the children. How old are your children?

ELISABETH  My son is 30 and my daughter is 23.

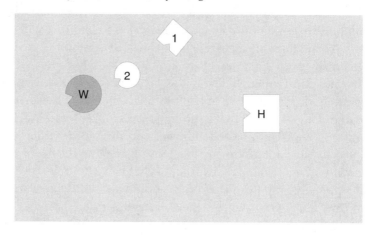

H  Husband
**W  Wife (Elisabeth)**
1  First child, a son
2  Second child, a daughter

HELLINGER  An awful picture!

ELISABETH  Yes, I don't really understand it.

HELLINGER  What's with your daughter?

ELISABETH  I'm afraid my daughter is taking over the responsibility.

HELLINGER  No, no. She's dying.

ELISABETH  Yes, she's following behind me.

HELLINGER  And your son is also following you.

ELISABETH  Yes, it looks like that here.

HELLINGER  Who does the death impulse come from?

ELISABETH  Right now, from me there.

HELLINGER  The death impulse comes from you.

*Hellinger moves the daughter next to her father.*

184

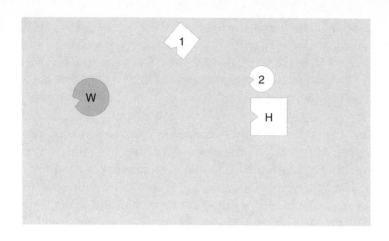

HELLINGER *to daughter* How's that?

SECOND CHILD I can breathe now. I felt like I didn't have any future.

HELLINGER Yes, exactly.

HELLINGER *to husband* And you?

HUSBAND I'm better now. I was very dizzy and was staring horror-stricken at my son the whole time.

HELLINGER *to son* And you?

FIRST CHILD Now I'm afraid. At first I would have followed gladly, but now I'm frightened.

HELLINGER Go and stand at your father's side.

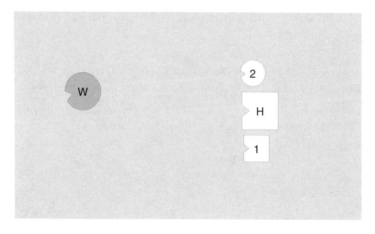

HELLINGER *to son* How is it now?

FIRST CHILD Yes, it's good.

SECOND CHILD  It's getting better.

HELLINGER *to Elisabeth's representative*  How are you feeling?

ELISABETH'S REPRESENTATIVE  For me, the closer I got to the void, the easier it was. I feel very free towards the front. My back is hot and cold. When my daughter was standing behind me, my hands got warm.

HELLINGER *to Elisabeth*  What happened in your family of origin?

ELISABETH  My mother didn't marry my father. My father was half Jewish. At first he couldn't get permission to marry, but then he did get it. He was a well-known artist and I think he got permission from Hitler himself. But then my mother refused him and didn't want to marry him. Because she had a career and was very involved in her work, she gave me away very soon. I had a lot of different caretakers. My mother was rejected by her family because in their circle it just wasn't done to have an illegitimate child.

HELLINGER  So, who was half Jewish?

ELISABETH  My father.

HELLINGER  That's very important, of course. Who does this disaster come from?

ELISABETH  From my father?

HELLINGER  No, no. Who does it come from?

ELISABETH  From me?

HELLINGER  No, no, you're the child. It comes from your mother. There's the Aryan, arrogant, moral superiority. And who does the blessing come from?

ELISABETH  From my father?

HELLINGER  From your father, exactly. Now place representatives for your mother and father. Place them according to your feeling.

186

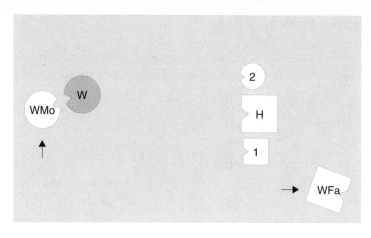

WFa    Wife's father, who was half Jewish
WMo  Wife's mother

*Hellinger then moves Elisabeth's representative somewhat to the side and puts her father in her previous position, with her mother opposite him.*

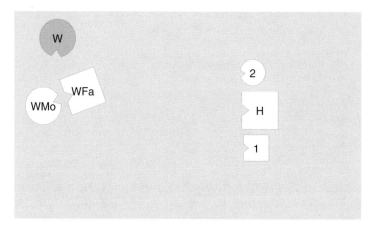

HELLINGER  That's it. Now it's getting serious.
*To mother*  Tell your husband, "I'll go instead of you."
WIFE'S MOTHER  I'll go instead of you.
HELLINGER  How does that feel?
WIFE'S MOTHER  I don't even know what I'm saying.
HELLINGER  How does it feel?
WIFE'S MOTHER  I have to say it again. I'll go instead of you. Yes, that's right.

HELLINGER  Do it.

*The mother moves off to the side. Hellinger moves Elisabeth's representative next to her father and asks the mother to turn towards them.*

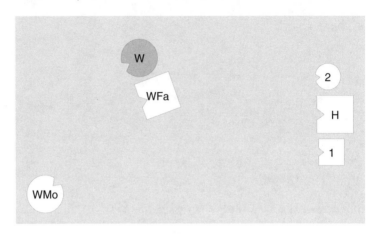

HELLINGER *to Elisabeth's representative*  Say, "Papa."
ELISABETH'S REPRESENTATIVE  Papa.

*The father puts his arm around his daughter.*

HELLINGER  "You're the right one."
ELISABETH'S REPRESENTATIVE  You're the right one.

*The father and daughter embrace warmly.*

HELLINGER *(after a while) to Elisabeth's representative*  How is it now?
ELISABETH'S REPRESENTATIVE  Ever since he came into the constellation, right from the beginning, there was so much warmth and love and such a big heart.
HELLINGER  How's the father?
WIFE'S FATHER  Good. Very good.

*Hellinger brings Elisabeth into the constellation.*

HELLINGER *to Elisabeth as she stands next to her father*  Say to your mother, "I'll go instead of you."

**188**

ELISABETH (*sighs*) I'll go instead of you.

HELLINGER How is that for you?

ELISABETH I don't know. Nothing.

HELLINGER How is it for the mother?

WIFE'S MOTHER Good.

HELLINGER *to Elisabeth* It's good for your mother.

*To father* Say to her, "You stay here."

WIFE'S FATHER You stay here.

*He puts his arm around Elisabeth and smiles at her.*

HELLINGER *to Elisabeth* Look at him.

*To father* Take her in your arms. The father has to be active here.

*The father takes Elisabeth in his arms and holds her tightly, although she resists.*

HELLINGER *to mother* What is it?

WIFE'S MOTHER I feel as though I have to go, or I'll draw her to me. I don't want her there. I'm envious. I want her to come to me. Standing here and watching, I can't stand it.

HELLINGER Here's the deadly one. The tragedy bearer is here. You still have to stand it a bit longer.

HELLINGER *to Elisabeth* Stand next to your father again. How are you feeling?

ELISABETH Not good. I'm totally stiff.

HELLINGER Okay, then stand next to your mother.

ELISABETH I don't want that, either.

HELLINGER Stand in front of your father now.

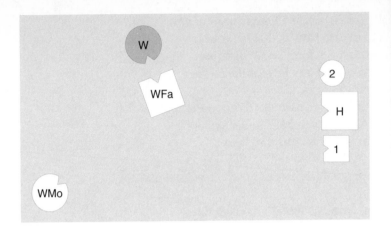

HELLINGER *to Elisabeth* Tell him, "I've scorned you." Say it to his face. "I've scorned you."

ELISABETH I've despised you.

HELLINGER "As my mother did."

ELISABETH *(sighs)* As my mother did.

HELLINGER "I've been ashamed of you."

ELISABETH I've been ashamed of you.

HELLINGER "And I've denied you."

ELISABETH Yes, I've denied you.

HELLINGER "Now, I'm sorry."

ELISABETH Now, I'm sorry.

HELLINGER How is that for the father?

WIFE'S FATHER I feel very open and I can let her in.

HELLINGER Exactly, fathers aren't so unforgiving. They let their children get away with things.

*To Elisabeth* Say to him, "Let me come to you."

ELISABETH But I don't trust him.

HELLINGER So it is. There's the scorn. "I don't trust you." There's the scorn.

HELLINGER How is the son feeling?

FIRST CHILD Not well at all. I've got backache.

*Hellinger moves him next to his grandfather.*

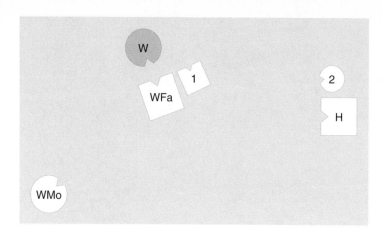

HELLINGER Tell your mother, "I love your father."
FIRST CHILD I love your father.
HELLINGER *to grandfather* How does that feel?
WIFE'S FATHER It's right. Good.
FIRST CHILD Yes.
ELISABETH Even if he doesn't even know him?
HELLINGER Even if he doesn't even know him, of course. He is a part of him. What do you think? His blood flows through his grandson, and his spirit moves in him. You could look at him that way.
*After a while* Now step back somewhat and kneel down. Kneel down and bow down to the floor with your hands stretched out, palms up.
*After a while* Now straighten up, but remain on your knees. Look at him and say, "I am a Jew."
ELISABETH I am a Jew.
HELLINGER Say it with love.
ELISABETH I am a Jew.
HELLINGER "Like you."
ELISABETH Like you.
HELLINGER How is that?
ELISABETH It's good.
HELLINGER Exactly. Now stand up again.

*Hellinger places Elisabeth, her father, and her son opposite her mother.*

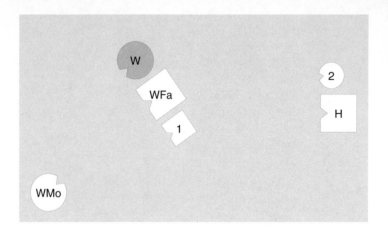

HELLINGER *to Elisabeth* Look at your mother and tell her, "I am a Jew."

ELISABETH I am a Jew.

HELLINGER "Like Papa."

ELISABETH Like Papa.

HELLINGER How is it now? Yes, her chest has puffed up.

*To mother* How are you feeling now?

WIFE'S MOTHER I won't get her now. Now, I'm the immoral one. Now, I'm all alone.

HELLINGER Look at your husband and tell him, "I've done you an injustice."

WIFE'S MOTHER I've done you an injustice.

HELLINGER "And I leave our daughter with you."

WIFE'S MOTHER And I leave our daughter with you.

HELLINGER *to Elisabeth* How is it now?

ELISABETH I'm sad.

HELLINGER Your mother has lost her rights. She's lost her right to belong.

*Hellinger turns Elisabeth, her father, and her son around. He moves her husband next to her and the children opposite their parents.*

192

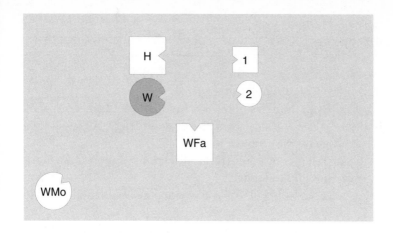

HELLINGER *to husband* How are you feeling?

HUSBAND I feel strength coming from the right side. Suddenly, I feel something different in my relationship to her.

HELLINGER *to Elisabeth* How is it for you now?

ELISABETH It's a good feeling to have my father there.

HELLINGER Tell him.

ELISABETH It's a good feeling to have you there.

HELLINGER "At last."

ELISABETH At last.

HELLINGER Now you can take your father in your arms. Now it will work.

*Elisabeth and her father embrace for a long while.*

HELLINGER *(after a while) to Elisabeth* Tell your children, "This is my father."

ELISABETH This is my father.

HELLINGER "A Jew."

ELISABETH A half Jew.

HELLINGER Say it to them.

ELISABETH This is my father, a Jew.

FIRST CHILD I'm really proud.

SECOND CHILD I love him. He brings so much strength.

HELLINGER *to Elisabeth* How are you?

ELISABETH I think this is good. I'm fine.

WIFE'S FATHER I'm also fine.

HUSBAND  Me, too.

HELLINGER *to Elisabeth*  Tell your husband, "I acknowledge that you married me."

ELISABETH  I acknowledge that you married me.

HELLINGER  "Even though I'm Jewish."

ELISABETH  Even though I'm Jewish. But that's not bad, is it?

HELLINGER  Just say it. I agree with you completely, but say it to him.

ELISABETH  That's no problem for me.

HELLINGER  Tell him one more time, "I acknowledge that you married me, even though I'm Jewish."

ELISABETH  I acknowledge that you married me, even though I'm Jewish.

HELLINGER  Do you know what you have replicated? Driving away your husband, just as your mother did.

ELISABETH  I didn't see that.

HELLINGER  Precisely. Now look at your husband and say to him, "I exonerate you."

ELISABETH  I exonerate you.

HUSBAND *(sighs)*  I hear it.

HELLINGER *to Elisabeth*  Now go and stand next to your father.

*To husband*  And you stand opposite your children.

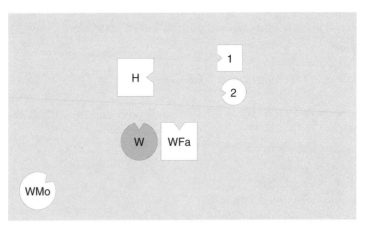

HELLINGER  That's the image of the resolution and that's where I'll leave it. Okay, that was it.

194

# Brigitte*
## Her father took over a business from a Jewish businessman

### SUMMARY

The entanglements: *Brigitte's father was a Nazi who took over a business from a Jewish businessman in Prague, who had been forced out. He has to follow this businessman, probably into death, but his daughter wants to go in his place. She also takes on the fears of the expelled businessman and behaves as though she has been condemned to a concentration camp, possibly like him. Brigitte's brother became schizophrenic and committed suicide.*

The resolution: *Brigitte stands next to the Jewish businessman and says to him, "My heart is with you. I acknowledge you and your fate with love." Brigitte's father feels calm when he is prepared to follow the Jewish businessman, who is also appeased by this. Only then is Brigitte able to turn to her husband. Both the Jewish businessman and Brigitte's father look upon the pair with goodwill.*

HELLINGER *to Robert, Brigitte's husband*  How are you?
ROBERT  I've come here alone. My wife is in hospital due to severe anxiety attacks. She's been there for some weeks and it's impossible to tell how long she will be there.
HELLINGER  We'll set up representatives for you and your wife first. In a collected way, choose two people and place them in relationship to one another.

---

* Course in Leipzig

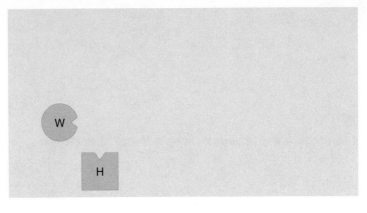

H   Husband (Robert)
W   Wife (Brigitte)

HELLINGER *to wife* How do you feel?

WIFE I'm looking straight ahead. I have no inclination to look at my husband.

HELLINGER *to husband* What about you?

HUSBAND I'd like to go to my wife.

HELLINGER What are your feelings?

HUSBAND Confused.

HELLINGER *to group* When you look at this picture, you can see that their visual fields don't connect.

*To Robert* The question is, where is each of them looking? Did anything special happen in your wife's family?

ROBERT Her parents are divorced. They separated after the war because her father continued to openly support National Socialism. He felt betrayed by his wife because she did a turn-about and took over full responsibility for the family. After that, he didn't have to concern himself with the family. During the war he had taken over a business in Prague that clearly must have belonged to a Jew. My wife has two brothers: the younger one became schizophrenic and committed suicide.

HELLINGER I'll set up some things connected to her family and we'll see what's there.

*Hellinger chooses representatives for Brigitte's father, for her younger brother who killed himself, and for the Jewish businessman.*

196

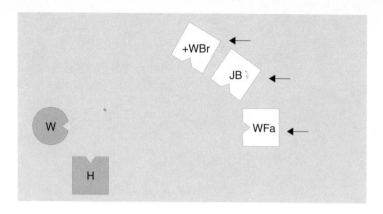

WFa  Wife's father
JB   Jewish businessman
WBr  Wife's younger brother, who committed suicide

HELLINGER *to wife* What has changed? Where do your eyes go?

WIFE To my brother. First I looked at each of them in turn, and now my eyes are only on my brother.

HELLINGER *to brother* How are you feeling?

WIFE'S BROTHER I don't really know. I look over there and feel chaos.

HELLINGER *to Robert* He was schizophrenic. The representative feels the confusion immediately.

*To father* What about you?

WIFE'S FATHER I feel a cold wall in front of me, and although I'm looking directly at my daughter, there's no relationship there.

HELLINGER What's over here to the right?

WIFE'S FATHER There's a relationship there. At least there's contact in that direction.

HELLINGER With the Jewish businessman or your son?

WIFE'S FATHER To both. At the moment I can only determine the general direction.

HELLINGER *to Jewish businessman* And you?

JEWISH BUSINESSMAN I can only look at one spot. My head is pounding, 'Oh, God; oh, God; oh God.' I'm very hot and I can only look at this one spot. I'm panicky on the inside and I'm standing here like a pillar of salt. It eases a bit when the father speaks.

HELLINGER *to father* I'll move you opposite him for now.

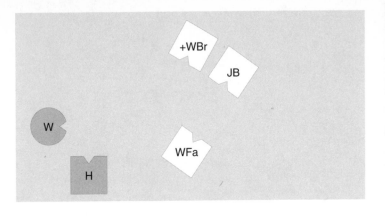

HELLINGER *to Jewish businessman* How is it now?

JEWISH BUSINESSMAN I'm simply frightened. I feel pushed backwards and I can't find my voice. I feel threatened.

HELLINGER *to father* And you?

WIFE'S FATHER I'm standing here rather calmly, with neither antipathy nor any particular attraction.

HELLINGER *to Jewish businessman* How is that?

JEWISH BUSINESSMAN He's very strong and stoical – very powerful. I see him as if he were much bigger than he is.

HELLINGER *to wife* What has changed for you?

WIFE Now I'm looking at the Jewish businessman. I'm very moved by seeing his distress.

HELLINGER Go and stand next to him.

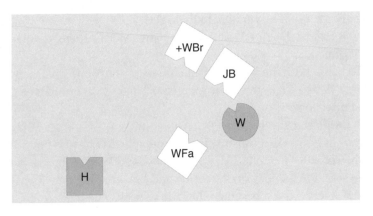

HELLINGER *to Jewish businessman* How's that?

JEWISH BUSINESSMAN  I'm very sad. That feels so good. Ah, that feels very good.

HELLINGER *to wife*  Tell him, "My heart is with you."

WIFE  My heart is with you.

HELLINGER  "I acknowledge you and your fate."

WIFE  I acknowledge you and your fate.

HELLINGER  "With love."

WIFE  With love.

HELLINGER *to Jewish businessman*  And how is it now?

JEWISH BUSINESSMAN  It's bad. When she was talking it was easier, but it's still bad and I feel like I have to go. I have to leave. But it makes up for something and it feels good.

HELLINGER  Okay, turn around.

*He turns around and Hellinger leads him a few steps further.*

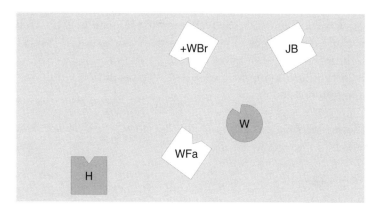

HELLINGER *to wife*  How is it?

WIFE  I'd like to go with him.

HELLINGER  Exactly.

*Hellinger places Brigitte's representative behind the Jewish businessman.*

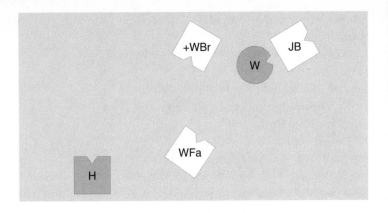

HELLINGER *to father* And who has to go?
*To husband (who's very emotional)* What's going on with you?
HUSBAND I'm sad. *(He sobs.)*
HELLINGER *to father* What about you now?
WIFE'S FATHER Ever since she went over to him–and now the feeling is getting even stronger – I've felt completely superfluous here. I feel so light that I could just move on out.
HELLINGER She's dying in your place. The resolution would be for you to follow him.

*Hellinger moves the wife aside and puts her father behind the Jewish businessman.*

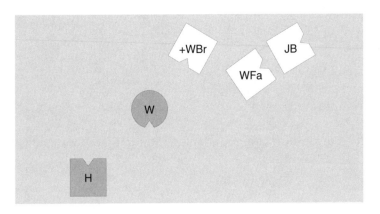

HELLINGER How is that?
WIFE'S FATHER Very relaxed and loose.

**200**

HELLINGER *to Jewish businessman* And you?

JEWISH BUSINESSMAN Before I was looking up to God and now with this I feel relieved, contrary to all my expectations.

HELLINGER *to group* He was most probably killed. We can assume that. The wife's father has to lie down with the dead. He has to leave the family and lie down with the dead. Then there is peace. Then they are both on the same level. Then, the woman will be free.

*To wife* Stand next to your husband.

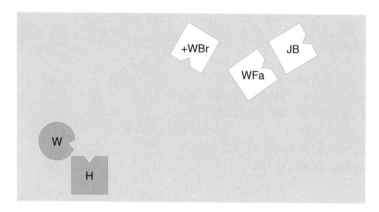

HELLINGER How is it now?

WIFE It feels good to see that he's touched.

HELLINGER *to husband* Put an arm around her. Yes, like that.

*The husband and wife put an arm around each other.*

HELLINGER *to brother* How are you feeling now?

WIFE'S BROTHER Fine. I don't notice anything special. I feel pushed a little bit backwards. But otherwise, it's cold.

*Hellinger has the husband and wife change places and puts the dead brother next to his sister.*

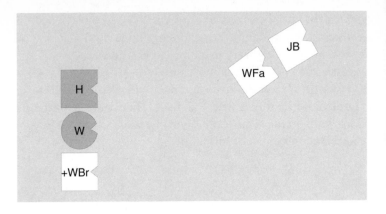

HELLINGER *to wife* How's that?
WIFE It's new, but interesting. *(She laughs.)*
HELLINGER *to brother* And for you?
WIFE'S BROTHER For me, too. It's getting warm next to me.
HELLINGER *to husband* And for you?
HUSBAND I feel calmer.

*Hellinger brings Robert into the constellation at his place. He spontaneously puts his hand on his wife's representative.*

JEWISH BUSINESSMAN *to Hellinger* Since you've moved the people behind me, something has changed for me. I feel like I have to look at them. Suddenly I'm filled with goodwill towards this woman, because when everything was very difficult, she gave me a spark of human warmth.
HELLINGER Turn around towards her.

*Hellinger asks the father if he would rather remain turned away from the others, or if he would prefer to stand next to the Jewish businessman. He chooses to stand next to the man.*

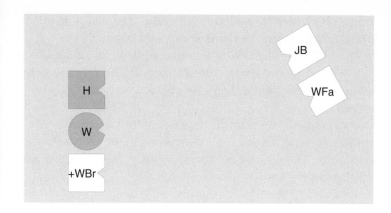

HELLINGER *to wife* How's that for you?

WIFE I really like that Jewish businessman over there.

HELLINGER The healing strength comes from him when he is respected.

*To group* I was told by Robert that two of his brothers died very young. I'll now add two representatives for his two brothers.

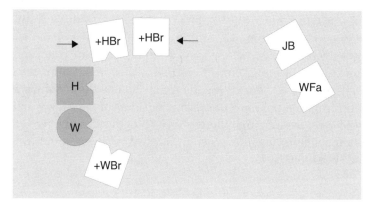

HBr   Husband's brothers, who died young

HELLINGER *to Robert* How is that?

ROBERT Yes, it's good to feel my brothers next to me.

HELLINGER *to wife* And for you?

WIFE I feel much better. *(She laughs.)*

HELLINGER *to group* The three dead people may stay with the living and bring blessings.

*(Indicating the Jewish businessman)* He's also dead, but when the father stands next to him, he changes and feels goodwill.

WIFE'S FATHER  That's true. With the changes that were made behind us as we stood turned away, things changed. The impulse to turn towards the others grew and now he's moved very positively in that direction.

HELLINGER *to Jewish businessman*  How is that for you now?

JEWISH BUSINESSMAN  It's easier for me to accept him. I feel something more like fate, now. When he says things like that, it's good and I could also forgive him.

HELLINGER  Okay, that's it.

## LOVE AND FATE

Hellinger *to group*  In a poem about Prometheus, Goethe wrote a line that reflects much of our current feeling about life. "Hast du nicht alles selbst vollendet, heilig glühend Herz!" (Oh, sacred, glowing heart, have you not mastered it alone?) That's what many believe about love. They say, "We can make it," and fail to recognize how intertwined they are in the destinies of others, or how these destinies continue to have effects. The effects continue until the carrier is acknowledged and the excluded are given a place. But when this is done, life and blessings come from them. Then, the heart can truly master and perfect. But before the reconciliation work is done and respect has been paid, the unfinished business of fate stands in the way of love. Even though there is love on both sides, the two partners cannot come together when unfinished business from the past stands between them.

# Preliminary Remarks*

This course took place in the large auditorium of the university with an audience of 600. The auditorium is located in what used to be the Jewish quarter of Hamburg, and a few hundred meters away is the former site of the great synagogue which was destroyed during "Reichskristallnacht", the night when Jewish businesses and places of worship were smashed and burned. There is now a large open area where the synagogue once stood and the outline of the synagogue is marked on the ground in remembrance.

Although this was offered as a general course in family constellations with ill patients, an unusually large number of those requesting constellation work were descendants of victims and perpetrators in the Third Reich. It was almost as if the place itself demanded that the dead be honoured and that they be allowed to bless their descendants in the task of bidding farewell to the horror and turning to their own lives. This is what occurred during the course, often in dramatic and moving ways.

At the end of the course, someone laid three roses on the stage in the name of all those present. A simple gesture, as if to bow down to the dead and their fate and to grieve with them.

* Course in Hamburg

# Eva[*]
## Half of her family were Jews who survived by being baptized

### Summary

The entanglements  *Eva's father and his family were Jews. They were, however, very proud of having converted to Christianity, which enabled them to survive. Eva's aunt was murdered in Auschwitz. Eva's deceased daughter was connected to this aunt.*

The resolution  *Eva tells her paternal grandfather, "I am a Jew." They embrace warmly. Eva's father says to both his parents, "I am a Jew." He embraces them. Eva's youngest daughter tells Eva, "I am a Jew like you." They embrace emotionally. Eva also says to her husband, "I am a Jew." As representatives are added for the murdered Jews, everyone bows before them, even Eva's mother. After that, Eva's mother can stand next to her Jewish husband. When Eva's aunt who died in Auschwitz comes into the constellation, Eva's deceased daughter stands next to the aunt and says, "This is where I want to stay." Eva tells her daughter, "I leave you there with love. I'll come too."*

HELLINGER *to Eva*  I'll begin with you.
*To group*  We've already talked with one another, so I have some prior information about her.
*To Eva*  Set up your present family: that is, your husband, you, and the three children, one of whom has died.

---

[*] Course in Hamburg

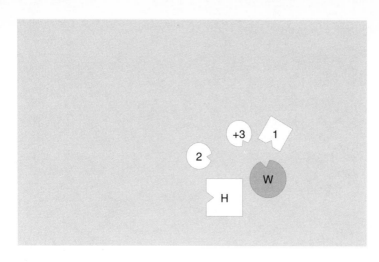

H  Husband
**W  Wife (Eva)**
1  First child, a son
2  Second child, a daughter
3  Third child, a daughter, who died at age 23

HELLINGER *to husband* How are you feeling?

HUSBAND I don't feel like I quite belong. As if I were being pushed away by my wife.

HELLINGER How does the wife feel?

EVA'S REPRESENTATIVE I feel terrible. I feel pressured by my son and my husband. This man is a total stranger to me. I want the second daughter to be gone. The youngest is the only one I like a bit. It's quite appropriate the way she's standing here. Mostly I'd like to be gone from here.

HELLINGER *to group* A picture like this one indicates that the children prevent the mother from going. How's the son doing?

FIRST CHILD I don't feel well. Something's pulling me backwards, I'd like to take about ten steps backwards.

HELLINGER And the second?

SECOND CHILD I feel a connection with my sister and have the impression that I don't really have much to do with the others.

HELLINGER The youngest?

THIRD CHILD I'm very calm and feel as if I weren't here, I'm untouchable.

*Hellinger places the children opposite the father.*

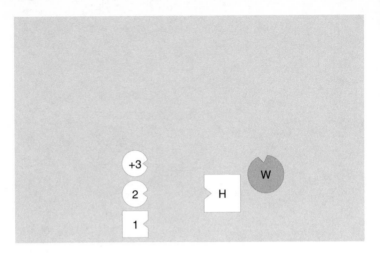

HELLINGER How's the wife now?
EVA'S REPRESENTATIVE I'd like to see where they're going. The pressure is gone, but I would still like to see where they are.

*Hellinger moves her next to her husband.*

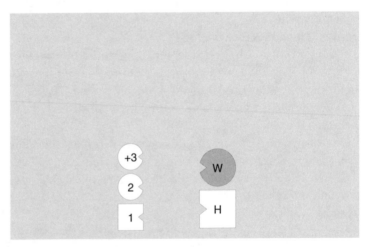

EVA'S REPRESENTATIVE This is much better here. I'm relieved.
HELLINGER How's the husband feeling?
HUSBAND Much better now. I've got a feeling of warmth and space.

208

HELLINGER  And the son?

FIRST CHILD  There's still a feeling of being drawn backwards, but it's better than before.

SECOND CHILD  I feel much better than before. Now, I can see those two as my parents. Before, I didn't have any relationship with them.

THIRD CHILD  I'm aware of the changes and I find them interesting, but only from a distance. Basically, not much has changed in my feelings.

HELLINGER *to Eva*  How do you feel looking at that?

EVA  Really, I'm just sad.

HELLINGER  There's a special circumstance in your family of origin. Would you briefly describe that?

EVA  Half of my family were Jewish. They were very proud that they had been baptized as Christians. We survived because we were baptized. Yes that's it. And so, here I stand today.

HELLINGER  Your father was Jewish?

EVA  Yes.

HELLINGER  Put in representatives for your father and his parents.

*Eva chooses three representatives and Hellinger places them in the constellation.*

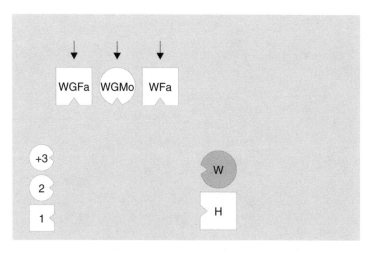

WFa   Wife's father, who is Jewish
WGF   Wife's grandfather (paternal)
WGM   Wife's grandmother (paternal)

HELLINGER  What has changed?

EVA'S REPRESENTATIVE  I'd like to have the grandfather behind my back, but not the other two.

FIRST CHILD  The pull backwards is gone. I feel like I can stay here.

SECOND CHILD  I feel as though I'm standing firmly on the ground.

THIRD CHILD  Not much has changed. There's still a fog around me and I still feel out of reach. There's nothing that can touch me.

HUSBAND  I'm now aware – but was already there before – that I feel like a distant stranger to my wife. That's better now that this side is filled in. It's slowly getting more complete and I've got a calm feeling in the middle.

HELLINGER  How's the wife's father feeling?

WIFE'S FATHER  I've got cold feet. At the same time, I feel like I really have to put in a lot of effort to hold my daughter.

WIFE'S GRANDMOTHER  I keep looking at my granddaughter, because she brought in the Jews, the true Jews.

HELLINGER  That's a reason that doesn't count here.

WIFE'S GRANDMOTHER  But I feel something in my belly.

HELLINGER  Okay, you're her grandmother, that's reason enough.

WIFE'S GRANDFATHER  I have a lot of sympathy for my family, especially for my son-in-law and my grandchildren.

EVA'S REPRESENTATIVE  I want to go over there. My back is cold. I feel drawn over there.

*Hellinger leads her to her grandmother and has her lean back against the grandmother.*

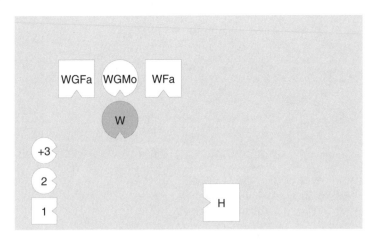

EVA'S REPRESENTATIVE  It's better now.

*The grandmother puts her arms around her granddaughter and holds her firmly.*

HELLINGER *to deceased daughter*  Has anything changed for you yet?
THIRD CHILD  It's pleasant, but it doesn't touch me.
HELLINGER *to Eva*  We need a representative for your mother.

*Eva chooses a representative and brings her into the constellation.*

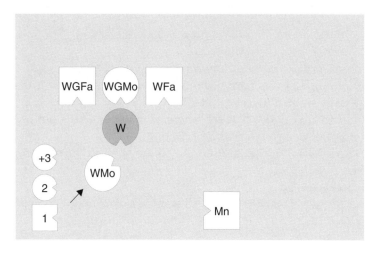

WM  Wife's mother

HELLINGER *to wife*  What has happened?
EVA'S REPRESENTATIVE  I feel completely happy here.
HELLINGER  What happened when she came in?
EVA'S REPRESENTATIVE  Nothing special.
HELLINGER *to deceased daughter*  What happened with you?
THIRD CHILD  Some interest, but not very strong. It was minimal.
SECOND CHILD  It seems strange that I can't see her. I'm aware that something isn't quite right with my right leg. That began somewhere along the way and it's a very strange feeling.
FIRST CHILD  When she came into the middle, my heart got warm.

*Hellinger moves the wife's mother next to her Jewish husband.*

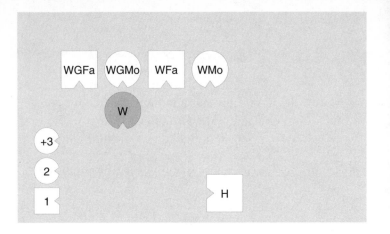

HELLINGER *to wife's mother* How was that for you?

WIFE'S MOTHER I was happy standing there alone. It wasn't that I necessarily wanted to leave, but I didn't feel very affected.

WIFE'S FATHER I notice that she's here, of course, but it's not ... *(he makes a qualifying gesture with his hand).*

WIFE'S MOTHER I'm cold and I'd like to move off to the side somewhat.

HELLINGER Yes, go.

WIFE'S MOTHER I want to be alone. I want to isolate myself, emphatically, like this.

*She stands off to the side with her back turned to the others.*

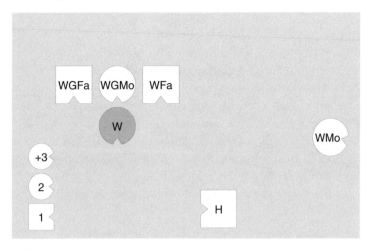

212

HELLINGER *to wife* How is it?

EVA'S REPRESENTATIVE I felt safer when she was here at my side. Now there's such a chill, because she's gone.

*Hellinger moves the wife next to her father.*

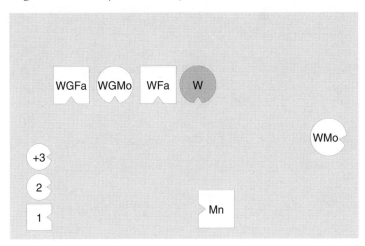

HELLINGER How's that?

EVA'S REPRESENTATIVE More comfortable. I can stand here. *(sighs)* I feel safe now that my grandmother has put her arms around me. Now I can stand.

*Hellinger brings Eva into the constellation, first next to her father and then in front of him.*

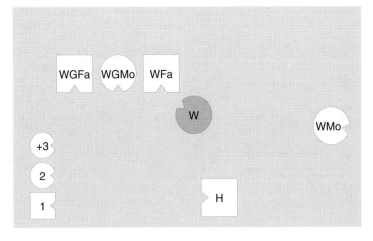

HELLINGER *to Eva* Take a moment to feel the situation.
*After a while* Look at your father and tell him "I'm Jewish."
EVA I'm Jewish.
HELLINGER Tell your grandmother too.
EVA I'm Jewish.
HELLINGER *to Eva (who is very moved)* Go to her.
*To grandmother* Take her in your arms.

*Eva and her grandmother embrace for a long time. Eva weeps.*

HELLINGER *(after a while) to grandfather* Follow your impulse.

*The grandfather moves behind the grandmother.*

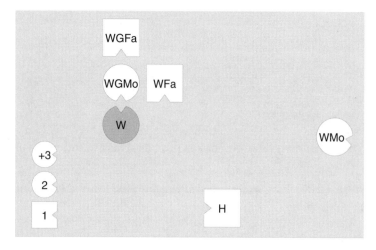

*Hellinger now moves Eva next to her husband and puts her father opposite his own mother. The grandfather returns to his place next to the grandmother.*

HELLINGER *to wife's father* Look at your mother and tell her, "I'm Jewish."
WIFE'S FATHER I'm Jewish.
HELLINGER How is that?
WIFE'S FATHER Good.
HELLINGER Go to her.

214

*He moves to his mother and embraces her.*

HELLINGER *(after a while) to wife's father*  Now tell your father, "I'm Jewish."
WIFE'S FATHER  I'm Jewish.
HELLINGER  "As you are."
WIFE'S FATHER  As you are.
HELLINGER  Go to him, too.

*He goes to his father and they embrace warmly. Then the grandfather, grandmother, and father stand next to one another.*

HELLINGER *to deceased daughter*  How are you feeling?
THIRD CHILD  I'm feeling more alive. There's a great sadness, and every time someone says, "I'm Jewish," I feel like saying, "So am I."
HELLINGER  Tell your mother that.
THIRD CHILD  I'm Jewish.
HELLINGER  "Like you."
THIRD CHILD  Like you.

*Eva goes to her mother for a long embrace. Both are very moved. Then they look into each other's eyes and embrace again. In the meantime, Hellinger chooses five representatives for murdered Jews and places them behind Eva's father and grandparents. Then he brings Eva back to her husband's side.*

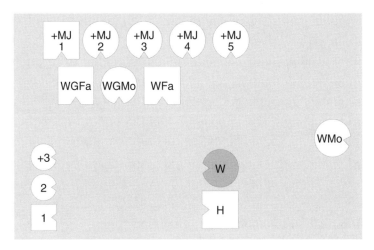

MJ 1   First murdered Jew
MJ 2   Second murdered Jew, etc.

HELLINGER *to Eva* Tell your husband, "I'm Jewish."

EVA I'm Jewish. *(She cries.)*

HELLINGER How is that for the husband?

HUSBAND It's good that she says that now, and that she's finally noticing me, and has something to say to me. This whole scene was difficult for me. Everyone had something in common, and I was an outsider. I had only the hope that I could find something in common with the children. Something new could be opened up there now.

EVA Yes, that's good.

HELLINGER How are you doing now?

THIRD CHILD I'm warm and I feel very light.

SECOND CHILD I felt very touched. More than anything, all of a sudden there were so many people there. Before that I hadn't had the feeling that I belonged, but when they all came in, that really changed.

FIRST CHILD I don't feel much connection with the family, but I suddenly feel as though I can stand on my own.

HELLINGER *(indicating Eva's relatives and the people standing behind them) to group* They survived, and the five behind them represent all those who were murdered.

*To father and grandparents* Turn around to the murdered ones.

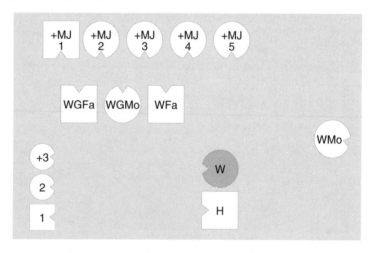

HELLINGER *to second murdered Jew* How is it?

SECOND MURDERED JEW I'm dead.

HELLINGER *to father and grandparents* Bow down before the murdered, all three of you. Bow deeply. Simply bow deeply.

HELLINGER *(afterwards) to second murdered Jew* What has changed?

SECOND MURDERED JEW I'm still dead.

HELLINGER *to first murdered Jew* And you?

FIRST MURDERED JEW At first my feeling was, I am dead, and also that there was something owed to me. As they bowed, that feeling was appeased somewhat. The deciding thing was when I looked over to the survivors and felt goodwill towards them. As the others bowed, I could see them over there.

HELLINGER *to father and grandparents* Now stand next to the murdered ones, in a semi-circle, so that you can see them.

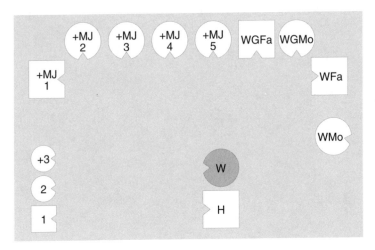

HELLINGER *to second murdered Jew* How are you now?

SECOND MURDERED JEW I'm beginning to come alive.

HELLINGER *to third murdered Jew* And you?

THIRD MURDERED JEW Before, it seemed good to me that at least a few had survived. Now it's really good.

FOURTH MURDERED JEW The way in front of me is so clear. I'm grateful.

FIFTH MURDERED JEW I'm very comfortable and I'm glad that some survived.

WIFE'S GRANDFATHER I feel very connected to my grandchildren.

WIFE'S GRANDMOTHER My heart's pounding and I'm very excited.

WIFE'S FATHER It's nice to have a connection here. On the side towards my wife, though, it's still cold.

HELLINGER *to wife's mother* How are you?

WIFE'S MOTHER It touches me a little, what's happening there, but I don't feel like I have any right to be there. *(Somewhat defiantly)* I feel fine here.

HELLINGER Now bow down before each of the murdered Jews and before your husband and his parents.

*She goes to each one and bows down in a collected and respectful way. As she comes to her husband, she says, "I'm happy to see him." Then she bows down to him and stands next to him.*

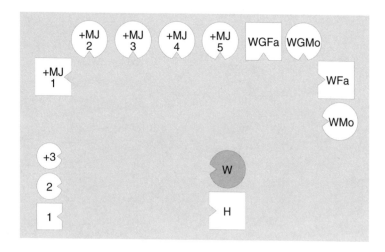

HELLINGER *to wife's father* How is it?
WIFE'S FATHER Now it's right.
WIFE'S MOTHER Ah yes, he is my husband.

*Hellinger places Eva and her husband so that they can see all the others.*

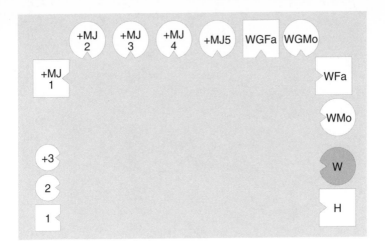

HELLINGER *to Eva* How are you feeling now?

EVA Very good.

HUSBAND I still feel somewhat on the edge and overwhelmed. I'm aware that something is happening there that's stronger and more powerful than me. I also feel that I didn't get enough, but I can't say anything about that because this other suffering is so monstrous and all-powerful. So I have to come to grips with a deep split at the moment.

FIRST CHILD I still have no connection to my parents, but I've suddenly gained two sisters. That's nice.

SECOND CHILD I saw that when my grandmother bowed down, my mother looked at my father very lovingly. That released something in me. Before that, I didn't have much of a connection with them, but now I see them as my parents.

THIRD CHILD I'd like to go over and join the dead. The rest seems meaningless in comparison with them. I have a special relationship to that woman there *(she indicates the second murdered Jew)*.

HELLINGER *to Eva* Do you know who that is? That's the aunt who was killed in Auschwitz.

*To deceased daughter* That's where you should go.

*She goes to the aunt and leans back against her. The aunt puts her arms around her and holds her.*

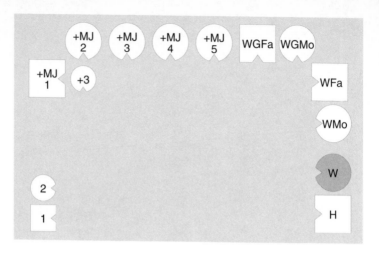

HELLINGER *to deceased daughter* How is it now?

THIRD CHILD It's soft and loving and calm. I'd like to stay here.

HELLINGER *to Eva* Exactly, she is lying with the dead. Tell her, "I'll leave you there."

EVA I'll leave you there.

HELLINGER "With love."

EVA With love.

HELLINGER "And I'm coming, too."

EVA And I'm coming, too."

HELLINGER Okay, that was it.

### FELLOWSHIP IN A SHARED FATE

Hellinger *to group* In this constellation, my information wasn't coming only from the picture in the constellation. I have also had many experiences over the past few years with patients and clients who have a Jewish background and I'd like to explain a few things about that work.

The dead are dead only when they are feared and, therefore, not respected. As soon as they are acknowledged, they come to life in their own way. The acknowledging here took the form of bowing down to them and the descendants declaring their Jewishness. Then the dead, who had been excluded through their fate, can return to the family. That has a healing effect.

I have seen many Jewish survivors who have a guilty feeling of being perpetrators. They have the same feelings as the perpetrators. They deny their heritage and the imagined offence by identifying themselves vehemently as Christians, or by devaluing that which is Jewish in the family. For example, her mother had devalued the Jewishness. The grandparents and father had themselves baptized and became good Christians. In doing so, they denied the community and destiny that they came from. That has a bad effect.

The healing way leads back to the excluded, in this case to the dead, to acknowledge them, grieve with them, join their company, and say to them, "I am your brother, I am your sister."

*To Eva*  And perhaps also, "Among you, I'm the little one." That's also a healing sentence that resolves and allows reconciliation. It's clear that a man who marries a woman with such a clan hasn't got a chance. Not because anyone is bad – no one here was bad. But, you found a good resolution at the end, so he can come to you.

# Isolde*
## Her grandfather shot Jewish women and children

### COMMENT

*This constellation has such density and fullness that it cannot be summarized. If you let it have an effect on you as a whole, you will be moved to the depths, particularly by the statements of the representatives of the murdered Jewish children.*

HELLINGER *to Isolde* What's the issue?

ISOLDE Ever since I've had children of my own, I've felt certain that I would die soon, and I don't want to.

HELLINGER Are you ill?

ISOLDE After my first daughter was born, there was a suspicion of breast cancer, but it turned out not to be. I have days when I'm convinced that I'm ill, but I don't go to a doctor. There's something hanging over me that I don't understand. *(She cries.)*

HELLINGER How many children have you got?

ISOLDE Two daughters, ages five and two.

HELLINGER They're certainly adorable, at that age. Okay, we'll set up your family your husband, you, and your daughters. Was either of you in a significant relationship before?

ISOLDE No.

* Course in Hamburg

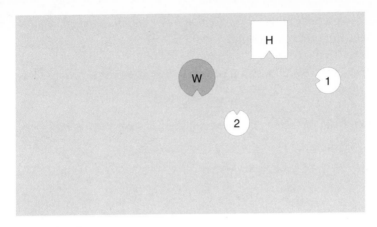

H   Husband
**W   Wife (Isolde)**
1   First child, a daughter
2   Second child, a daughter

HELLINGER *to Isolde* When you look at that, it's clear that you're looking at someone who's not there. Who is that?
ISOLDE I'm looking into the past, at my father and my grandfather.
HELLINGER What happened to them?
ISOLDE My father committed suicide when I was a year old, and my grandfather was in the SS and shot Jewish women and children.
HELLINGER Add representatives for the two of them.

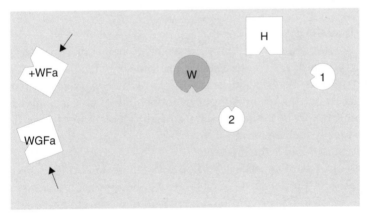

WFa   Wife's father, who killed himself
WGFa  Wife's grandfather, who was in the SS and shot Jewish women and children

HELLINGER *(indicating the representatives for the father and grandfather) to Isolde* But you're not looking at them.

ISOLDE That's true.

HELLINGER Now choose ten people to represent the murdered Jewish children.

*When Isolde has chosen the representatives, Hellinger places them opposite the family.*

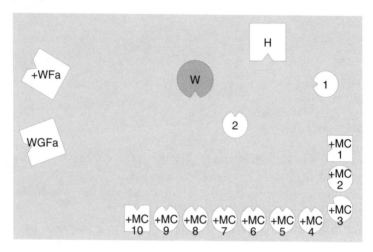

MC1 First murdered child
MC2 Second murdered child, etc.

HELLINGER *to wife* How do you feel?

ISOLDE'S REPRESENTATIVE Not very well. My hands are tingling and cold, and my legs are very shaky. I can see one daughter, but I can only see the other one out of the corner of my eye. I feel like I need support, but there's no support from behind. I can't feel anything behind me, or to the side. I have a need to look at my father, but I can't really feel anything.

HELLINGER How is the husband?

HUSBAND I want to get my children out of there and bring them over to me, and I feel a mixture of sadness and aggression towards my wife. She should turn around and this all makes me angry.

HELLINGER How is the elder daughter?

FIRST CHILD I feel lost. I can see my mother, but she doesn't see me. My father's too far away, and I'd like to go over there.

HELLINGER *to younger daughter* And you?

SECOND CHILD I felt all alone. When the Jewish children came in, I had an urge to go and join them.

*Hellinger moves the wife and children next to the husband.*

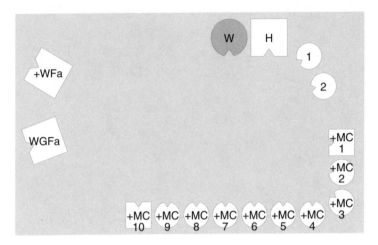

HELLINGER *to wife's father* How do you feel?

WIFE'S FATHER Ever since I've been standing here my arms have felt very heavy and my hands are like ice. The space in front of me is wonderful and open. I don't feel anything about what's been happening behind me. I haven't got any contact.

HELLINGER Stand next to your daughter.

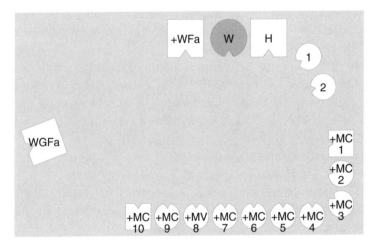

HELLINGER *to wife's grandfather* And how do you feel?
WIFE'S GRANDFATHER Like I'm dead. I'm only on call.

*Hellinger turns him towards the dead children.*

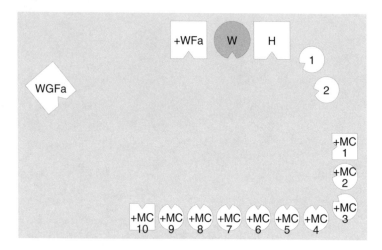

HELLINGER *to wife* How is it now?
ISOLDE'S REPRESENTATIVE I'm getting warmer on my left side. My children are still too far away. I'd like more contact with my husband, but I'm aware that something isn't reaching me, or I need something that I'm not getting.
HELLINGER *to Isolde* She doesn't feel for the dead children. She hasn't even looked at them or mentioned them at all. *(Isolde nods.)* In this way, she's like her grandfather. He doesn't look at them, either. Does that make sense?
ISOLDE It makes sense in my life at the time before I knew what my grandfather was and what he had done. I was a very cold child. But through my own experiences, and finding out what happened, things have changed. Now I don't know if I'm good or if I'm evil. *(She is very emotional.)*
HELLINGER Come and take your place in the constellation.
*To wife's father* How are things with you?
WIFE'S FATHER I don't have any contact to my left. I'm only aware of some very nasty looks coming towards me – very threatening, like a tribunal.

226

HELLINGER *to group* He's innocent and he's taken over something for his father. He took the punishment on himself by committing suicide.

*To husband* How are you feeling, now?

HUSBAND The aggression is gone. I'd like to take my family and turn around and leave.

HELLINGER You can't get out of it that easily, that doesn't work. You can't simply turn away.

*To Isolde* Lie face down in front of the dead Jewish children.

*She lies down in front of the dead children and cries.*

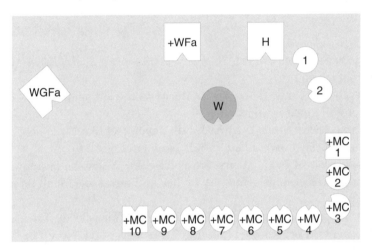

HELLINGER *(after a long pause) to Isolde* Now get on your knees.

*To her children* And you kneel down on either side of your mother.

*To all three* All of you look over there.

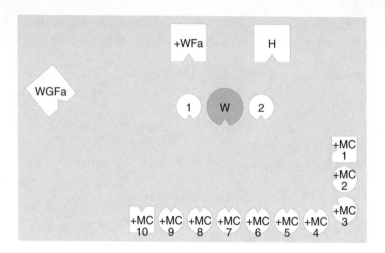

HELLINGER *(after a while) to the representatives of the dead children* How is that for you?

FIRST JEWISH CHILD There's a solidarity to the left, and sadness and goodwill towards this family.

SECOND JEWISH CHILD At first I didn't even feel like I was here and when she lay down, I had to sigh. Now I'm fine.

THIRD JEWISH CHILD At first I was ice-cold. When she lay down, I started to feel some sympathy for her, and now I feel for all three of them.

FOURTH JEWISH CHILD I was cold at first, too. When she lay down, and then got on her knees, I thought, "This feels good. Now I've been acknowledged. That's in order."

FIFTH JEWISH CHILD When the younger daughter said what she did, I shuddered. This isn't right yet, I still don't feel good. It's not enough.

SIXTH JEWISH CHILD I'm glad that I'm not standing here alone. I feel touched that she's looking at us and is aware of us.

SEVENTH JEWISH CHILD When she lay down, I got very sad, but also more alive. But, it still isn't enough.

EIGHTH JEWISH CHILD At first the family didn't matter to me at all. The only thing that was important to me was this one *(the grandfather)*, although I noticed I couldn't look at him. I was only aware that he was standing there. As things went on, I first got sad, and then furious. That's got somewhat better since she lay down, but it wasn't an immediate change. It's a good thing it lasted a while. But, it's still not right.

228

NINTH JEWISH CHILD  At first I was cold and dizzy and I didn't feel like there was consideration for me. When she lay down, I got warm. I'm still dizzy, though.

TENTH JEWISH CHILD  At first I was clearly dead, but when she lay down, that feeling dissolved. At the moment I feel a combination of bottomless grief, and deathly fear from this side (*indicates grandfather*).

HELLINGER *to grandfather*  How are you doing?

WIFE'S GRANDFATHER  As she was lying there, I would have liked to lie down, too, but I'm not certain if I'm allowed to do that, if I have any right.

HELLINGER  Do it. Lie down here where you're standing, in the direction of the dead children.

*After a long while to fifth Jewish child*  How is that, now?

FIFTH JEWISH CHILD  There was some relief as he lay there. It's not over yet, but it's better now that he's gone – that he's also dead on the floor.

EIGHTH JEWISH CHILD  I need to turn away from that.

HELLINGER *to the dead Jewish children*  All of you turn away. I'd like to see how it is if you all turn.

*They all turn their backs, although the seventh Jewish child resists doing so.*

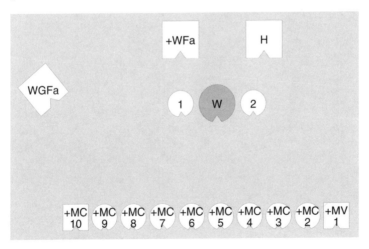

HELLINGER  How is that?

FIRST JEWISH CHILD  It's more comfortable.

Second Jewish Child  A relief.

Third Jewish Child  I felt some pity for him and wondered what had made him so hard. It doesn't really matter which way round I stand.

Fourth Jewish Child  I feel better.

Fifth Jewish Child  I'd like to see what's there.

Sixth Jewish Child  I'd also rather turn around. I liked it that he was lying on the floor.

Seventh Jewish Child  I'd like to turn around, too. I want him to look me in the eye. It's not good to keep your eyes closed.

Eighth Jewish Child  Now there are so many other people there.

Ninth Jewish Child  I feel better. I felt rather angry when he lay down.

Tenth Jewish Child  When he lay down, I got some contact with those three *(the wife and her two children)*. I'm sorry that's gone.

Hellinger  Now turn back around, all of you.

*To grandfather* Stand up. How was that for you?

Wife's Grandfather *(sighs)* In a way, I felt better lying there. That in spite of everything, I could still have some way to exist somehow …

Hellinger  No, that you don't have. Leave the room and close the door behind you.

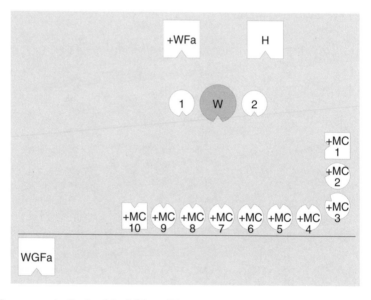

Hellinger *to the Jewish children* How is it now?

Tenth Jewish Child  I can breathe and my backache is disappearing.

Ninth Jewish Child  I'm fine.

EIGHTH JEWISH CHILD  For the first time, I've got some interest in this family.

SEVENTH JEWISH CHILD  I need eye contact with someone.

SIXTH JEWISH CHILD  My back cracked.

FIFTH JEWISH CHILD  It's better, but now I'm aware of the younger daughter and I think the mother has to do something. Something has to happen that both honours us and ends this.

FOURTH JEWISH CHILD  I'm glad that he's gone. I watched him go and wasn't sure if he'd really go. I didn't feel happy until the door had closed. Then, I felt calmer and immediately looked at the mother. I thought, "Now, something has to happen."

THIRD JEWISH CHILD  The cold is gone. I feel alive again and I'm waiting for something.

SECOND JEWISH CHILD  I wasn't sure that he would go, and I was glad when he did. Now I've got a firm ground to stand on and I have pity on the mother.

FIRST JEWISH CHILD  My attention is back on the family.

HELLINGER *to husband*  How was that for you, all that time?

HUSBAND  I had an urgent need to kneel down. I got in contact with the dead children and I wanted to kneel down or bow down.

HELLINGER *to wife's father*  And you?

WIFE'S FATHER  That was a lot. First I felt this tribunal, which was very difficult for me. That got easier when my daughter lay down. At that moment though, I was aware that the dead children were looking down at her. I thought, "No way! I can't allow that." I wanted to stand in front of those three to protect them, but I had to just bear it. That only eased up when he lay down on the floor and my tension let up because my children and grandchildren were out of danger. When he left, it was good for me. When they all turned around, I had the urge to join them, in the same direction.

*Hellinger moves the wife's father next to the dead Jewish children. He has the wife and her children stand up and moves her husband next to them.*

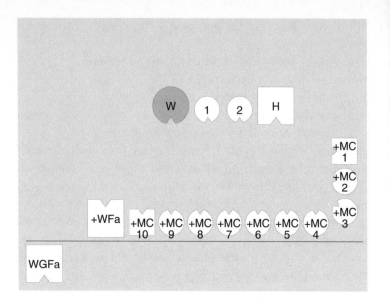

HELLINGER *to the parents* Now take your children by the hand and bow down deeply, with love. Put a hand on your heart.

*After a while* Now straighten up.

*To husband* Say to them, "Please."

HUSBAND Please.

HELLINGER *to Isolde* You say the same to them.

ISOLDE Please.

HELLINGER How is that for you?

ISOLDE I still have the feeling that I have to go there. *(Sobs)*

HELLINGER Stand next to your father.

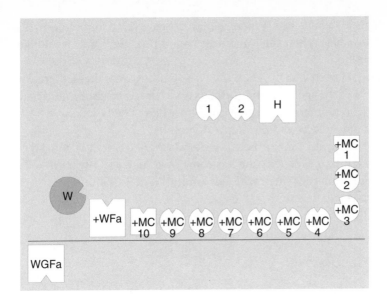

HELLINGER *to Isolde* How's that?

ISOLDE I feel like that's what I deserve. It's a relief.

HELLINGER *to the dead Jewish children* How is that for you?

FIRST JEWISH CHILD Death seems like something very impersonal to me, as though it has nothing to do with my murderer, and certainly nothing to do with his granddaughter. For me, it's inappropriate for her to stand here, she ought to be with her family. I'm not interested in her atonement. That's not up to her.

SECOND JEWISH CHILD My knees got weak when she came over. My first thought was that she doesn't belong to us.

HELLINGER It's presumptuous to stand with the dead when you don't belong there.

THIRD JEWISH CHILD It's simply too much.

FOURTH JEWISH CHILD I don't want this sacrifice, that's not her place.

FIFTH JEWISH CHILD For me, she's got a job to do with her children, to try to put an end to the suffering.

SIXTH JEWISH CHILD I felt very sad. She doesn't need to follow us and her father, her place is with her family.

SEVENTH JEWISH CHILD If she'd look at me, she'd know that she can't stand here.

EIGHTH JEWISH CHILD I feel warmer. She means something to me.

NINTH JEWISH CHILD When she lay down, I felt a lot of goodwill towards her. When she came over here, I thought, "You don't belong here."

TENTH JEWISH CHILD When she was standing over there, there was a lot of exchange back and forth, a very close connection, and I had an urge to help her. When she came over here, I felt aggressive.

HELLINGER *to wife's father* How do you feel?

WIFE'S FATHER I'm fine here. I've felt very good since I've moved over here. It pains me that she has come over here and I want to tell her that her place is there with her family. I'll do this alone.

HELLINGER Exactly.

*To Isolde* Now go back.

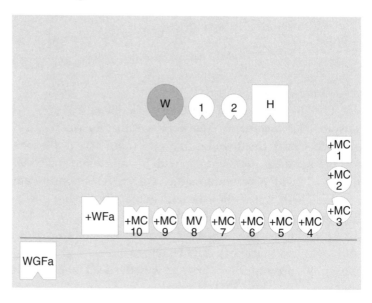

HELLINGER *to Isolde* Now look each of them in the eye.

*After a while* How is that? *Isolde shakes her head.*

Tell them, "After a while, I'll come, too."

ISOLDE After a while, I'll come, too.

HELLINGER Now, look at your children and tell them, "Now, I'll stay a while longer."

ISOLDE Now, I'll stay a while longer. I'll stay a while longer.

HELLINGER Tell your husband, too.

ISOLDE I'll stay a while longer.

234

HELLINGER I'll leave it there. It's difficult for everyone, but that's the way it is.

*Hellinger has the grandfather come back into the room.*

HELLINGER *to wife's grandfather* How was it out there?
WIFE'S GRANDFATHER I was glad that you said I had to leave. I felt very relieved. I wouldn't and couldn't stay here, and that's how I felt out there. I'm also glad to be relieved of this role.

HELLINGER *to group* It was moving to see the multi-faceted way the representatives of the Jewish children could experience this and to see so many different aspects of that which is healing.

*To the representatives* I'd like to thank you especially. It was very moving for me, the way you expressed yourselves, particularly what the representative of the first dead child had to say about death. Death is impersonal, and there's something else beyond it, something greater. I believe that it's only in this larger picture that one can respect and do justice to the greatness of this fate and the effects that emerge out of it.

# Erika*
## Her parents hid a Jewish woman

### Letter of October 20, 1997

*Dear Bert,*

I need to tell you about my experience taking part in the seminar in Hamburg, and to ask for your advice.

Even during that weekend, I couldn't let go of the image of those ten Jewish children. Inside myself, I also bowed down before them, and through this constellation, I found a freeing affirmation that history can come to rest in such a way. Resolution is possible.

Without knowing why, I had been very occupied with this theme ever since I was 20 years old. I read and watched everything I could get a hold of, and brought it all into a youth group I was leading at the time. Then, when I began my university course in Catholic theology, we read the books *"Gott in Auschwitz"* and *"Gott ist tot."* My beliefs and my picture of the world collapsed, and for a long time nothing came in its place. From that time on, I didn't want to see or hear anything more about the Holocaust.

In my family it was never talked about, with the exception of one conversation that I remember. When I was about ten years old, my mother, who is German, told me how awful it had been when they were living in Poland and the SS came to take the Jews from their homes, including her neighbour. My mother had hidden a Jewish woman. I don't know any more than that and can't ask because my parents are both dead. Until yesterday, I hadn't though much more about it.

---

* Postscript to Hamburg Course

For the past ten years I've frequently got into a state of panic at night, in terror that someone would break in and kill me or us. I get absolutely paralyzed. Gradually, over time, I've learned what to do when it happens. I do relaxation exercises and put myself in God's hands, and that helps somewhat.

Every once in a while I've had the feeling that it isn't my fear, but I've never really found a solution. Last night the stories from Hamburg kept going through my head every time I woke up, and somewhere I remembered this story that my mother had told me. The sentence came to me, "This fear belongs to the Jewish woman that my mother hid."

My intellectual understanding doubts what my body experiences. Whenever I think about the connection to this Jewish woman, my hand get sweaty, my heart pounds, and I get very agitated.

I remember a fragment of an example from you that had to do with a Jewish woman who stood shaking behind a door. Unfortunately, I can't remember the resolution.

Is it sufficient to bow down to her?

With love and thanks,
*Erika*

## REPLY LETTER OF OCTOBER **27, 1997**

*Dear Erika,*
What you have described makes sense. In this case you would let the Jewish woman go to her relatives and bow down before their fate. You yourself would return to the sphere of your own destiny and connect with the suffering person at a higher level. At a higher level one is connected and also free.
Best wishes,
*Bert*

# Jakob*
## "I am a Jew"

### COMMENT

*This constellation is also so dramatic that a summary cannot do it justice.*

HELLINGER *to Jakob* What is your issue?

JAKOB I am physically not very present in my life. I don't feel bad, but there's somehow something amiss. I don't experience myself as real, as if everything were a phantom.

HELLINGER What happened?

JAKOB I don't know very much about my family. My actual family of origin is very small, besides me, there's my brother and my mother.

HELLINGER What about your father?

JAKOB He died when I was nine months old.

HELLINGER From what?

JAKOB Leukaemia.

HELLINGER That's a critical event. Are you married?

JAKOB No.

HELLINGER Have you got any children?

JAKOB No.

HELLINGER We'll set up your father, your mother, and the two children. Which position are you in the family?

JAKOB I'm the younger son.

HELLINGER Okay, set it up.

When Jakob has selected the four representatives, he can't remember who is to represent whom in the constellation, and Hellinger has to clarify it for him.

* Course in Frankfurt, Germany

238

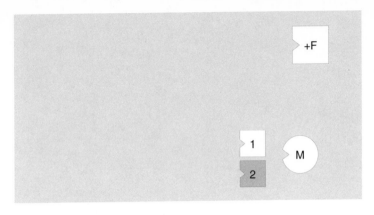

+F  Father (died when Jakob was nine months old)
M   Mother
1   First Child, a son
**2   Second Child, (Jakob)**

HELLINGER  Did your mother grieve when your father died?

JAKOB  I don't know.

HELLINGER  What would you guess?

JAKOB  I think she suffered quite a lot, physically, but I couldn't really say anything about what she suffered in spirit.

HELLINGER  What do you mean by physical suffering?

JAKOB  She told me once that it was so bad for her after my father died that she only weighed 38 kilograms.

HELLINGER  Your father has no place with the rest of you.

JAKOB  Right. I didn't know for a long time that such a thing as a father even existed.

HELLINGER  And this image, with the two sons standing in front of their mother–do you know what that indicates?

JAKOB  No.

HELLINGER  The sons are preventing their mother from dying or killing herself.

JAKOB  *very affected* Yes.

HELLINGER  A strange picture.

*To father*  How is the father doing?

FATHER  I feel a strong pull into death and I want to take their mother with me.

*Hellinger moves the sons next to their father.*

HELLINGER *to Jakob's representative* What's happening with you?

JAKOB'S REPRESENTATIVE I don't want to look over there. I'm contracting and making myself small. I'm pulling in so I don't see anything over there. That has nothing to do with me.

HELLINGER *to first child* And for you?

FIRST CHILD I'm still looking straight ahead. There was a lot of warmth and love over there. I also couldn't look at my father here. Even though I'm standing right here, I'm barely aware of him.

HELLINGER *to Jakob* There are some secrets here. It was also odd that you couldn't remember who the people were representing.

JAKOB A major problem in my life generally, is that I have trouble remembering things.

HELLINGER There are secrets. What was actually true? Is this really your father, or was there another man?

JAKOB It's terrible imagining he wasn't my father.

HELLINGER I can't do anything here. I haven't got any information, and without information, everything evaporates.

JAKOB I can only add that since I was young I have been looking into my grandfather's history. I feel very drawn to my grandfather.

HELLINGER Who's father is he?

JAKOB My father's father.

HELLINGER What happened to him?

JAKOB I think it must have been a very difficult thing on my father's side, because my grandfather was Jewish.

HELLINGER Ah, now it's coming out.

JAKOB Although that's not exactly true, because I found out recently that he was a so-called baptized Christian of Jewish origin, which is somewhat different.

240

HELLINGER The baptism doesn't make any difference here. I will add a representative for the father's father. Now we have the key figure.

*Hellinger puts the representative for Jakob's grandfather in the place where the elder son had been looking.*

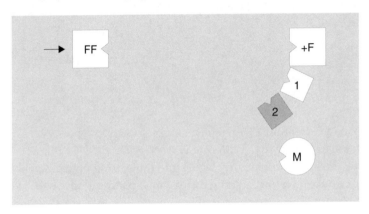

FF    Father's father (a baptized Jew)

HELLINGER *to father* How is it now?
FATHER I feel good here. I was already feeling fine when my elder son moved closer to me.
HELLINGER *to elder son* And for you?
FIRST CHILD It's wonderful. I can feel a tremendous warmth flowing out to this man.
HELLINGER *to Jakob's representative* And you?
JAKOB'S REPRESENTATIVE I would like to turn around. I wanted to do that even before he was in there. I could imagine myself moving backwards towards him.
HELLINGER Do that.

*Hellinger guides him backwards to his grandfather*

HELLINGER *to group* They're ashamed of their Jewishness, this family.
*To Jakob's representative* Turn around and look at your grandfather.

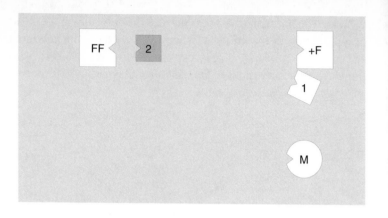

HELLINGER Tell him, "I am a Jew."

JAKOB'S REPRESENTATIVE I am a Jew. *(He exhales audibly.)* Phew! Now some life is coming into my face. Huh, I'm getting bigger. *(laughing)* The cramped feeling is going away. I'm expanding now.

HELLINGER How's the grandfather?

FATHER'S FATHER I'm also a Jew. *(They smile at each other.)*

HELLINGER *to Jakob* What do you have to say to that?

JAKOB It's not true for me. I would like to be, but I'm not.

HELLINGER Stand in front of your grandfather. Look him directly in the eye, and say, "I am a Jew."

*Jakob hesitates for a long time and begins to smile*

HELLINGER Yes, something is coming to life after all. Look at him and say that to him. *(As Jakob looks at Hellinger)* Look at him. I'm not important here.

JAKOB I can't quite look at him. Not yet.

HELLINGER Say it. "I am a Jew." You have to look at him to get clarity. *(As Jakob continues to struggle with himself)* Tell him, "I am not and will never be."

JAKOB *(laughing and shaking his head)* Well, actually …

HELLINGER Okay, then tell him, "I'm a Jew."

JAKOB *to his grandfather* I would like to be a Jew like my father.

HELLINGER Tell him, "I am one."

JAKOB I can't feel it.

HELLINGER Say it once anyway, just to be one the safe side. It won't hurt anything.

242

JAKOB To be on the safe side, I can say it. *(He laughs.)*
*To his grandfather* I am also a Jew. I am a Jew.
HELLINGER That's the truth. Exactly. Now move back a bit and lay down on the floor in front of him, flat on your belly, in the sense of giving him honour and respect. You don't have to say anything.

*In the meantime, Hellinger chooses five representatives for Jewish victims and places them behind the grandfather.*

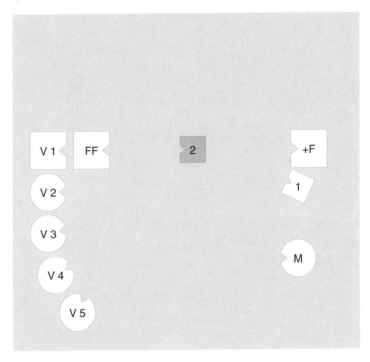

V1   First victim, a man
V2   Second victim, a woman
V3   Third victim, a woman
V4   Fourth victim, a woman
V5   Fifth victim, a woman

HELLINGER *to grandfather* What's happening with you?
FATHER'S FATHER Pain and grief.
HELLINGER I'll put you next to them.

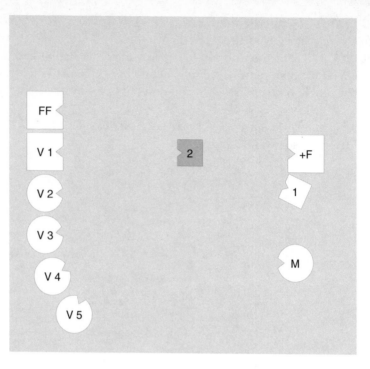

*As the father's father moves next to the first victim, he puts his arm around the man and lays his head on the man's shoulder. The victims move closer together and clasp hands.*

HELLINGER *to Jakob, after a pause* Now get up and stand next to them.

HELLINGER Look over at the victims and tell them, "This is my place."

JAKOB This is my place.

HELLINGER "My place is with you."

JAKOB My place is with you.

HELLINGER How are you feeling now?

JAKOB I'm very agitated, but I feel very real.

HELLINGER Exactly. How is the grandfather doing now?

FATHER'S FATHER Very well. I've found my peace here. When he says that his place is here, that is lovely.

HELLINGER *to first victim* And for you?

FIRST VICTIM I'm very touched, but he can only stay here for a short while.

HELLINGER Yes, of course.

FIRST VICTIM For the moment it's right, but the row ends here with his grandfather. I can feel that.

HELLINGER Exactly.

*To father* Now take both your sons by the hand and go forward and bow down before your father and each of these victims. Stand in front of each one and the three of you bow very deeply. And also, look each one in the eye.

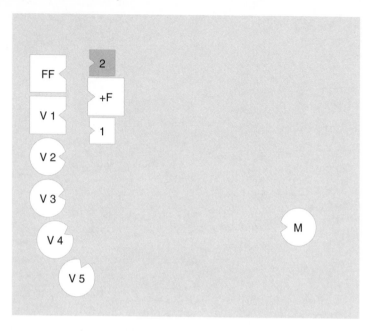

*The father and his two sons bow down in front of Jakob's grandfather, who responds by embracing Jakob. They continue to bow down to each of the Jewish victims. Each one acknowledges the honour. Then, the father stands next to his father, and the two sons stand next to their mother.*

HELLINGER *to Jakob* How are you feeling now?

JAKOB This doesn't feel good. I feel dizzy. This doesn't feel good at all here.

*Hellinger leads him in front of his father.*

HELLINGER Look at your father and tell him, "I have missed you very much."

JAKOB *(very moved)* I have missed you very much. I have missed you very much.

HELLINGER "Please look on me as your son."

JAKOB Please look on me as your son.

HELLINGER "And I take you now as my father."

JAKOB And I take you now as my father.

HELLINGER *to father* Take him in your arms.

*Jakob's father takes his son in his arms.*

HELLINGER *to Jakob as he embraces his father* Now take your father into your heart. Breathe deeply and take him into yourself. *After a while* Take a step back, look at him and tell him, "In me you are still here."

JAKOB In me you are still here. Yes.

HELLINGER "I will hold and respect this for as long as I am granted."

JAKOB I will hold and respect this for as long as I am granted.

248

HELLINGER  How do you feel now?

JAKOB  I feel right. Solid.

HELLINGER  And the father?

FATHER  I'm happy and a bit sad still. I'm getting happier all the time.

HELLINGER *to Jakob* Now move slowly backwards, looking at him all the while. Move very slowly, and keep the eye contact.

*Jakob moves back and returns to his place next to his mother.*

HELLINGER  Take your mother's hand.

*To mother* How are you doing?

MOTHER  Better now. Before I was drawn so strongly to my elder son. I didn't want the second son, but I wanted the first son all for myself.

HELLINGER  Tell them, "I'll keep both of you."

MOTHER  I'll keep both of you. Now I can see my husband for the first time.

HELLINGER *to Jakob* How do you feel now?

JAKOB  I feel very threatened. I don't feel well.

HELLINGER  Who feels threatened?

JAKOB  My father, I think.

HELLINGER  Exactly.

*Jakob holds his breath as if in panic.*

HELLINGER  Go to your brother.

*Jakob's elder brother holds him firmly in his arms. Then, Jakob returns the embrace. In the meantime, Hellinger has selected three male representatives and places them in the constellation.*

HELLINGER *to group* These are representatives of the murderers.

*To the elder son* You and your brother go and stand in front of them.

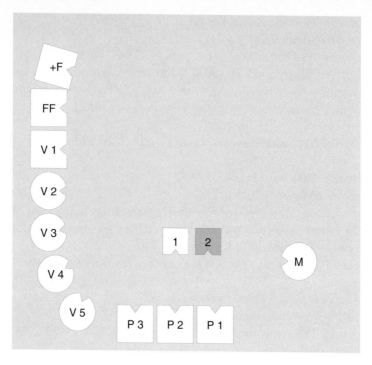

P1   First perpetrator
P2   Second perpetrator
P3   Third perpetrator

HELLINGER *to the brothers* Look at them and say, "We are Jews."
JAKOB Oh, my God. *(He trembles in fear.)*
HELLINGER Say, "We are Jews." Say it together.
JAKOB I can't do that.
HELLINGER Say it.
FIRST CHILD We are Jews.
JAKOB Yes. *(He is fearful.)*
HELLINGER Look them in the eye.
JAKOB Who are they?
HELLINGER They are representatives of the murderers. Tell them, "We are Jews."
JAKOB *haltingly* We are Jews. We are Jews.
HELLINGER "And we remain Jews." Tell them that.
JAKOB *fearfully* We remain Jews.
HELLINGER *to first perpetrator* How is that?

**250**

FIRST PERPETRATOR  Terrible

HELLINGER  Yes, that it is.

SECOND PERPETRATOR  It's true. Everything that is, is true.

THIRD PERPETRATOR  I could only settle down when he had said that.

HELLINGER *to the two brothers*  Go and stand next to your father again. Look over at the victims again and say, "We are Jews."

JAKOB *with great difficulty and fear*  We remain Jews – forever and ever.

FIRST CHILD  We remain Jews.

HELLINGER *to Jakob*  How is that for you?

JAKOB *still with anxiety*  I have some weight, somehow. It's terrible, but it's right.

HELLINGER  I'll put your mother alongside you now.

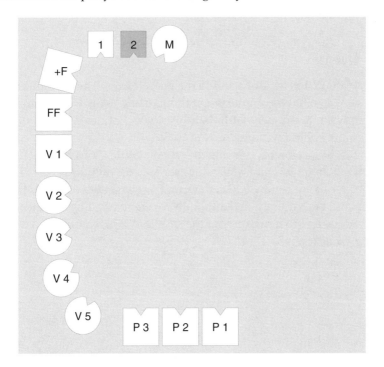

HELLINGER *to mother*  Tell your two sons, "I love your father in you."

MOTHER  I love your father in you.

HELLINGER  "And I respect him as a Jew."

MOTHER  And I respect him as a Jew.

HELLINGER  Is that sentence true?

MOTHER  Yes.

HELLINGER *to Jakob* It will take a long time for that to heal in the soul, but it's good. Agreed?

JAKOB Yes.

HELLINGER That was it then.

## JEWISH FATE

HELLINGER *to group* The Jewish fate, especially here in Germany, is very difficult. You can see how difficult it is and how difficult also for the descendants to declare themselves in that fate and stick by it.

*As another participant tries to comfort Jakob* No, don't touch him. Leave him be. You can't interfere with this. He is in safe hands now. He is in safe hands with the Jews.

## EPILOGUE

I bid farewell to the dead and to the perpetrators. They are entitled, as we are, to have even the worst things come to an end eventually. Then we, too, can deal with their history as Lot dealt with Sodom, leaving it behind without looking back.

But, as Jacob who, crossing the Jabbok, couldn't leave his accompanying angel without a blessing, we too can only leave the dead when we have acknowledged them and received their blessing. Then they pull back quietly, and although we are marked by the encounter, we are free to move on over the river that separates us from them for a while longer.

© Milly Orthen

Bert Hellinger is probably Europe's most innovative and provocative psychotherapist and a best-selling psychotherapy author. A former priest and a missionary in South Africa for 16 years, as well as an educator, a psychoanalyst, body therapist, group dynamic therapist, and family therapist, he brings a lifetime of experience and wisdom to his work. The family constellations, which have become the hallmark of Hellinger's approach, as well as his observations about systemic entaglement and resolution, have touched the lives of thousands of people and have changed how many helping professionals carry out their own work.

# Publications by/about Bert Hellinger and his work

In English these books are available:

**Love's Hidden Symmetry. What Makes Love Work in Relationships**
Bert Hellinger/Gunthard Weber/Hunter Beaumont *1998*
>   *352 pages. ISBN 1-891944-00-2*
>   *Carl-Auer-Systeme Verlag and Zeig, Tucker & Theisen, Inc.*
Bert Hellinger, Gunthard Weber and Hunter Beaumont have collaborated to present a beautiful collage of poetry, healing stories, transcripts of psychotherapeutic work and moving explanations of the hidden dynamics and symmetry love follows in intimate relationships. Original and provocative enough to change how you think about familiar themes.

**Love's Own Truths. Bonding and Balancing in Close Relationships**
Bert Hellinger/Gunthard Weber/Hunter Beaumont *1998*
>   *464 pages. ISBN 1-891944-48-7*
>   *Carl-Auer-Systeme Verlag and Zeig, Tucker & Theisen, Inc.*
Love's Own Truths represents another important milestone in the search toward an even greater understanding of the intricacies of relationship and resolution. Bert Hellinger describes „Love's Own Truths" as a fundamental statement of his approach

**Touching Love. Bert Hellinger at Work with Family Systems.**
**Documentation of a Three-Day-Course for Psychotherapists and**
**their Clients** *1997*
>   *186 pages. ISBN 3-8967 0-022-7*
>   *Carl-Auer-Systeme Verlag*
Bert Hellinger demonstrates the Hidden Symmetry of Love operating unseen in the lives of persons suffering with serious illness and difficult life circumstances. This book is a full documentation of a workshop for professionals held near London in February, 1996.

**Touching Love (Volume 2 ).**
**A Teaching Seminar with Bert Hellinger and Hunter Baumont** *1999*
>   *256 pages. ISBN 3-89670- 122-3*
>   *Carl-Auer-Systeme Verlag and Zeig, Tucker & Theisen, Inc.*
*This book contains the written documentation of a three-day*-course for psychotherapists and their clients. It offers mental health professionals and interested non-professional readers a look in slow-motion at Bert Hellinger and Hunter Beaumont at work.

**Acknowledging What Is. Conversations with Bert Hellinger** *1999*
>   *162 pages. ISBN 1-891944-32-0*
>   *Zeig, Tucker & Theisen, Inc.*
Deepen your understanding of Hellinger's transformative ideas on the »Natural Orders of Love« with his latest work - a moving dialog between the tough-minded journalist and the »Caretaker of the Soul«.

**Supporting Love. How Love works in Couple Relationships.**
**Bert Hellinger's Work with Couples**
Edited by Johannes Neuhauser 2001
> *279 pages. ISBN 1-891944-49-5*
> *Zeig, Tucker & Theisen, Inc.*

„In this expertly edited book, Johannes Neuhauser brings an artist's eye to Bert Hellinger's unique approach, and shows that beneath the surface of his often-startling work there is a gentle tenderness that calls - softly und steadily - to the truths that lay resting in our hearts. It is refreshing in this era of psychotherapeutic relativism to come across the work of a therapist who takes a quiet and clear-sighted stand for the centrality of love in human life. The power of the work that has emerged from Hellinger's unwavering focus on the flow of love in relationships is remarkable; it will touch any who come into contact with it - professional und lay readers alike." (Arthur Roberts, M.A., Editor und Co-Director, The Gestalt Press)
The english edition of »Wie Liebe gelingt«

**To the Heart of the Matter. Brief Therapies**
Bert Hellinger 2002
> *256 pages. ISBN 3-89670-396-X*
> *Carl-Auer-Systeme Verlag*

Bert Hellingers's particular brand of brief therapy can be very brief indeed. Perhaps truth needn't be long-winded, just seen. Translated by Collen Beaumont. The english edition of »Mitte und Maß. Kurztherapien«

**Insights. Lectures and Stories**
Bert Hellinger 2002
> *138 pages. ISBN 3-89670-281-5*
> *Carl-Auer-Systeme Verlag*

This is a first collection of Bert Hellinger's lectures and stories now translated into English. In this book he allows us to confront without fear the deep issues of guilt and conscience and brings to light the hidden orders through which love within and between people and groups succeeds. These stories attempt to lead us to a peaceful centre - a place where we can be collected and calm, in touch with our deepest love and longing, in tune with the world, and from which our relationships can be fulfilled and our lives healed. This is a book of wisdom: exciting, moving and profound.
The english edition of »Die Mitte fühlt sich leicht an«

**Images of the Soul.**
**The Workings of the Soul in Shamanic Rituals and Family Constellations**
Daan van Kampenhout 2001
> *156 pages. ISBN 3-89670-231-9*
> *Carl-Auer-Systeme Verlag*

Daan van Kampenhout and Bert Hellinger had a lengthy and intensive correspondence concerning the relation between shamanism and family constellations. The ideas explored in this correspondence formed the foundations of Images of the Soul, in which the dynamics of Hellinger's systemic work are carefully described from the viewpoint of tradional shamanism. The book points out those spiritual principles which lie at the foundation of both shamanic practice and family constellations, and includes many practical tips for people involved in systemic work as participant or trainer. Theoretical explorations are made concrete by examples from sessions with clients and groups, by personal experiences of the author with rituals on Indian reservations in the USA and by anecdotes from his studies with traditional medicine people and shamans.

The english edition of »Die Heilung kommt von außerhalb«

**The River Never Looks Back.**
**Historical and Practical foundations of Bert Helinger's Family Constellations**
Ursula Franke 2002
  *176 pages. ISBN 3-89670-391-9*
  *Carl-Auer-Systeme Verlag*

"The River Never Looks Back" is a book about the theory and practice of the method of systemic family constellation. Ursula Franke provides a well-grounded historical overview of the precursors to family con-stellations. In addition, she presents and defines the central termi-nology of these methods. The author presents a hypothetical model that attempts to explain the efficacy of con-stellations and deals with a number of questions that emerge when actually carrying them out. The empirical section of the book allows the reader to take a look at the procedure that is used in the process of a constellation, from the therapist's initial hypotheses to the resolution stage of the constellation. Franke explains, step-by-step, the application in individual therapy. In addition, the possibilities for and limitations of using constellations in individual therapy are discussed. The study presented in "The River Never Looks Back" focuses on therapy with anxiety patients. The results of the study can be used in regular psychotherapeutic practices, and is thus is helpful for all therapists who work with constellations.

**The Art and Practice of Family Constellations.**
**Leading Family Constellations as developed by Bert Hellinger**
Bertold Ulsamer 2002
  *198 pages. ISBN 3-89670-398-6*
  *Carl-Auer-Systeme Verlag*

Using the systemic family therapy developed by Bert Hellinger, tensions and conflicts within families can be revealed. Through the use of representatives, the person involved can observe the psychic dynamics of his or her own family, and identify the patterns which are destructive. In his book, Bertold Ulsamer explains the basis of family constellations, considers the task and the role of the therapist in the field of subjective experience and objective knowledge. He addresses the use of language and the issue of dealing with emotions. His book is aimed at therapists and others who are interested in the practical applications of the Hellinger therapy.

The english edition of »Das Handwerk des Familien-Stellens«

For more titles and to place your order please see:
# www.carl-auer.com